PEOPLE IN PROCESS

People in Process

The Preschool Years

MAXINE HANCOCK

Fleming H. Revell Company
Old Tappan, New Jersey

Scripture quotations identified KJV are from the King James Version of the Bible.

Scripture quotations identified NAS are from the New American Standard Bible, Copyright © THE LOCKMAN FOUNDATION, 1960, 1962, 1963, 1968, 1971, 1973 and are used by permission.

Excerpt from "Teach Your Child to Watch Television" by Maxine Hancock is reprinted by permission from the June, 1974, issue of MOODY MONTHLY. Copyright 1974 Moody Bible Institute of Chicago.

In Canada this book is being published by
G. R. Welch Company, Ltd., Toronto, Ontario.

Library of Congress Cataloging in Publication Data

Hancock, Maxine.
    People in process.

    Includes index.
    1. Children—Management. 2. Children development.
I. Title.
HQ772.H323   649'.123   78-17580
ISBN 0-8007-0947-0

FOR
*Sheryn and Allen
and my lovely godchild
Kori*

Contents

7

Acknowledgments

I have just typed the benediction on the last page of this manuscript. And now I turn it over to other readers.

But first, some thank-you notes:

To my family, of course. Without their loving encouragement and cooperation, there could be no books written here.

To my friends, especially those with very young families, who have posed the questions I have tried to answer in this book, and who have urged me to my work.

To Kathy Kent, my "summer secretary" who typed several drafts of this manuscript. Without her ability, energy, and enthusiasm, I could not have completed the manuscript at this time.

To those who read and reacted to various drafts, giving me important feedback: Isabelle Johnson, dear friend and young mother; and Marg Jones, my sister-in-love who read the entire manuscript; Mic and Linda Jacejko, creative young parents and educators, who reacted to the chapter "Creativity and Crafts"; and Betty Jorgensen, educator and mother, who interacted with me on "Creativity and Language." My deepest thanks for your contributions and insights—and above all, your encouragement.

To *Moody Monthly* for permission to reprint my article "Teach Your Child to Watch Television," which forms part of chapter 11, reprinted from the June 1974 issue of *Moody Monthly*.

Above all, I am thankful to God for having entrusted to me a ministry of words. "Let the words of my mouth . . . be acceptable in thy sight, O Lord, my strength, and my redeemer" (Psalms 19:14 KJV).

MAXINE HANCOCK

Introduction:
Why This Book?

Today, much is being written on parenting, by many authorities with as many different theories. Parents are becoming bewildered and confused by the cacophony of voices crying, "Do this! Do that!"

It is a strange thing, really. Not long ago, all you had to do to become a parent was to have a child. Now we have a verb "to parent," and in order to do that, we need all kinds of professional coaching. The task of parenting has been made so vastly complex, so endlessly difficult, so unbelievably demanding, that we have almost lost our nerve. When the field of parenting becomes the territory of psychologists, sociologists, educators, and psychiatrists, the feeling develops that the tasks of parenthood are so difficult, sensitive, and significant, that maybe they are best left to trained professionals.

But difficult, sensitive, and significant as the tasks are, it is time for parents to assert their right and responsibility to raise their children under God and for God. While gratefully acknowledging the insights of the professionals, we need to remind ourselves that from time immemorial, parenthood has been for amateurs—and the amateurs who have done the job best have been those who had confidence that it was their job to do.

Like all parents everywhere, I am an amateur. With four children born within five years, I have had an intensive crash course in early-childhood development. And I write for amateur parents—to encourage them to have confidence in their God, confidence in themselves, and confidence in their children. Confidence that it is a natural thing for parents and children to interact. Confidence that it is right and normal for parents to guide the development of their young. Confidence that it is necessary for parents to share their values with the new generation, "That the generation to come might know, even the children yet to be born . . . that they should put their confidence in God" (Psalms 78:6, 7 NAS).

Writing about family is a bit like trying to stuff the springs back into a clock you have taken apart. Everything keeps "sproinging" out—especially when you are in the midst of family living while you write. But I have chosen to focus on three key areas of personal development during the preschool years:

1. Confidence
2. Character
3. Creativity

I see *confidence* and *character* as the two great pillars on which *creativity* can be built—as the necessary prerequisites to meaningful creativity.

While these emphases will be of importance to all parents, not only Christian ones, I will be concerned with pointing out the ways in which a biblical Christian orientation promotes this threefold development—and how, in turn, children raised to have confidence, character, and creativity can contribute to the Christian community as well as to society at large.

When our first child was about three, he showed a sudden interest in our wedding picture. He studied the picture carefully, noting the long, white dress and veil I wore. Then he commented, "Her look like an angel. But her not an angel. Her is my mummy." How right he was. I'm not an angel—just a mother. And my children are not angels—just kids. I write from the crucible of very human family experience, with a full share of failure and discouragement together with satisfaction and deep joy. I write only because I believe that the family is God's plan, the most beautiful single evidence of His love. I believe that the Word of God reveals the necessary guidelines for the effective functioning of the family. And I believe that "the wisdom that is from above" (James 3:17 KJV) is supplied to trusting and obedient parents as they undertake the task of developing attitudes of trust and obedience in their children.

PEOPLE IN PROCESS

1

Beginnings

We are keenly aware that being parents demands the very best any of us has to offer.

"All beginnings are hard," says the midrash. But no beginning is any more difficult than the first few weeks of family life. Learning to live with a new and demanding member in the family is a challenge to the full resources of any couple's love.

I remember how it was with us. We had heard, of course, about the adjustments in marriage occasioned by the birth of the first child. But we were sure our love was strong enough, our marriage secure enough, our lives mature enough to see us through. We had been in love since we were teenagers; we had been married for over three years; we were well into our twenties. We had planned and prepared for parenthood, and had eagerly looked forward to our baby's birth. And even then those first weeks were tougher than anyone had suggested to us.

The new sense of being completely responsible for the welfare of a helpless little human weighed in on us immediately. For me, it was a clear intuition, "Now I'll never again be free of care," that put early youth forever behind. For Cam, the awesome sense of responsibility settled in as he brought us home from the hospital. He matured into fatherhood suddenly and visibly. I remember being startled to see a new look on his face, handsome as always under his crinkly dark hair, but now marked with a new gravity. There was a seriousness in his gray eyes that made him a mature-looking man. We had married young, and the early years of our marriage were spent in "palling around" together. Now, girlhood and boyhood were forever past. Having a baby was, for both of us, an aging crisis.

And when, after the first week, I came down from an ecstatic

17

emotional high, I came down hard. In fact, in the weeks of weariness and depression that followed, I wondered if there was any
bottom to how far down I would go.

Part of the problem was learning to share Cam. While many
writers note the husband's jealousy of the wife's close relationship with the new baby, the real jealousy problem in our marriage
was mine. I was jealous of the time and attention Cam lavished on
our newborn. Cam was an ideal father: holding, rocking, talking
to the baby at every opportunity. Never was a child more lovingly
accepted and claimed as son than Geoffrey. But the companionship I had cherished was diverted to our son.

Another point of conflict developed. Cam had been tender and
considerate during my months of pregnancy. Now, suddenly, he
was impatient and demanding. He wanted life to get back to
normal—and soon. When, during the baby's second week, I rejected Cam's suggestion that we invite friends over for supper, his
frustration boiled over into anger. "Don't you think you're making just a bit much out of this whole thing?" he asked.

I could hardly believe my ears. It wasn't like Cam. Suddenly
my heart felt empty of everything but resentment. I stood at the
bedroom door and watched Cam lean tenderly over the baby's
basket as he let the tiny fingers curl tightly around his own. A
fierce, deep anger kindled within me.

While I longed for more strength and rebelled against my
weakness and weariness, I also felt angry at the lack of understanding and acceptance being offered by a husband who had
been, before all else, my best friend.

Then came the night of Scrambled Eggs on Toast.

There was an unspoken judgment in Cam's eyes as he watched
me begin supper preparations that night. And it didn't help that I
was struggling with feelings of self-condemnation as I cracked the
eggs into the frying pan. How many nights of macaroni-and-
cheese dinners, wieners and beans—and now, scrambled eggs—
should a man have to put up with? I struggled with fatigue, too.
And with strung-out nerves. My hands were so shaky that, as I
cracked an egg, a piece of shell floated on the white. "Can't you
even crack an egg?" Cam asked as he turned away.

It was the "even" that got me. And suddenly my mind was

made up. This was a time for an understanding. I scrambled the
eggs, piled them on toast, and announced, "Supper," in a taut
voice. "You can say grace," I suggested. "That way you can eat
while I talk. I have to explain some things to you."

Cam bowed his head, and then looked up. "I don't think I
could pray right now," he said. "You had better talk first."

Commanding my nerves to be steady, refusing the tears that
were pricking at the back of my eyes, I locked my hands together
on the table in front of me.

"Cam," I said, "I love you very much. You were wonderful to
me while I was pregnant. But now I am finding you critical and
unsympathetic. And this is a time when I just can't take it. I want
to tell you something. You are a man. And you don't know one
little thing about what it takes to bear a child. A person cannot be
stretched to the absolute limits of elasticity—physically and
emotionally—and just go *snap!* right back into shape. You seem
to think I should be able to pick up where I left off before I got
pregnant. I'm telling you that I can't. I don't know what's wrong.
I don't know if it's normal. But I'm telling you—it's *me*. I need
your help now—not your criticism."

Cam listened carefully, then reached his hands across the table
and placed them over mine. "I didn't know," he said. "I'm
sorry." He paused, then went on. "But I think you need to be a
bit more understanding, too."

I looked at him sharply, stiffening defensively.

Cam went on. "You've got to remember something, Maxine.
This is my first baby, too."

Love flowed like a current between us, and we bowed our
heads for thanksgiving. Cold scrambled eggs on toast, complete
with flecks of shell, became a love feast, a celebration of our
having broken through to each other again.

It was on this basis of honest confrontation and open communication that we launched our most important endeavor in life: that
of being parents.

Three more times we would bring a baby home from the hospital; three more times we would work out the adjustments a new
life demanded—new adjustments, it seemed, each time. Camille,
a tiny, pink rosebud of a girl, joined our family seventeen months

after Geoffrey's birth. Geoffrey had been so robust and sweet tempered, I had mistakenly credited myself with model motherhood. Cammie-Lou changed all that—as wild as she was winsome, she was often sick, always demanding. When, two years later, we brought Heather Ruth home, we moved from being a neat, tidy, "convenient" family to being a real, unmanageablesized one. More than one apiece, now, to get ready for outings. Heather Ruth came, blessedly, as a sunshiny little smiler who could tease before she could talk. Mitchell was born just fifteen months later, and again we had two babies at once.

And now, our children are no longer babies. Geoffrey is almost twelve; Mitchell, at six, has just started school. The girls are ten and eight. Our children's preschool years are behind us. We're middle adults with a school-age family—and with all the teen years still ahead. So we don't pretend to be experts. We've only just begun—and we know that. But we *have* begun.

We have treasured the busy, exciting, demanding years with babies and preschoolers—as we treasure now the bustling years with a crowd of growing children around us. We share out from those years—not as superparents but as fellow travelers with other parents of preschoolers.

We are keenly aware that being parents demands the very best any of us has to offer. With our own resources often spent by midday, we are thrown hard upon resources of love and wisdom and strength which come only from our Father in heaven, the Prime Parent. Again and again we have to learn from His Word how best to love and train our children.

Part I

CONFIDENCE

Very often, confidence is the single greatest difference between the mediocre and the exceptional; between the joy of service and the pain of it; between looking life in the eye and running from it to hide.

There are three great sources of confidence—both for ourselves and for our children. These are laid out in chapter 2. In chapter 3 we look at our children and their potential from a biblical perspective. Then, in chapters 4, 5, and 6, we look at some practical ways in which confidence can be built into our children.

2

Confident Parents/Confident Kids

What is the difference between the approach of our grandparents and of ourselves in disciplining children? Whatever grandfather did was done with authority; whatever we do is done with hesitation. Even when in error, grandfather acted with certainty. Even when in the right, we act with doubt.

DR. HAIM GINOTT
Between Parent and Child

A young pastor's wife wailed to me, "How am I supposed to develop confident children? I have no confidence myself!" She spoke the part of thousands of parents today. Psychologist-author Dr. James Dobson speaks of an "epidemic of inferiority" in contemporary society.[1] And Christianity does not automatically provide immunity.

In fact, the tragedy of lacking adult confidence is nowhere seen more sadly than in our churches. We have people who spend their lives bound up in self-consciousness when they could be freed by confidence. People with leadership skills who cannot be persuaded to lead. People who live selfishly instead of servingly because they cannot be convinced that they have anything meaningful to give. Everywhere we look, we find the good gifts of God lying dormant; talents buried in napkins instead of being put to work in the service of God; creativity undeveloped; critical faculties stifled; love unexpressed: all for lack of confidence.

And the tragedy is self-repeating, for parents who fail to have confidence in themselves produce confused, nonconfident children, perpetuating the cycle of unused abilities, of God's work in this world being robbed of energy.

Very often, confidence is the single greatest difference between the mediocre and the exceptional; between the joy of service and the pain of it; between looking life in the eye and running from it to hide. Confident parents can produce confident kids—but where should an adult begin in a quest for confidence?

There are three great sources of confidence—both for ourselves and for our children. *First, there is the confidence that comes from acting under the authority of God's Word.* This kind of confidence can flow into the life of one who applies the Word of God in all areas of life. "The entrance of thy words giveth light; it giveth understanding unto the simple" (Psalms 119:130 KJV). An older generation who believed implicitly that the Bible was wholly trustworthy in every incidental teaching as well as in its primary focus did not dither as we do. "All scripture is given by inspiration of God, and is profitable . . ." (2 Timothy 3:16 KJV) is a rock upon which parents can ground their confidence, living in obedience to the Word of God, as it applies to the training of our children, as well as to the saving of our souls.

We cannot, of course, obey God's Word without having discovered it for ourselves. Lip service given to its authority and inspiration will never replace daily attentive reading and diligent study. The fact is that the Bible is saturated with family truth, from the very moment of the creation of man. I challenge parents to read their Bible through, marking the passages dealing with family in one color throughout—and then to reread the marked passages to draw out conclusions and applications. For a helping hand in studying relevant Scriptures, I would recommend Andrew Murray's classic *How to Raise Your Children for Christ*. It is a book that parents of young children could read together, carefully and prayerfully, and probably more than once. Some of the psychology contained in the book may be passé, but the spiritual principles are timeless and foundational to successful Christian parenthood.

Perhaps there is no confidence for parents like that which comes from the assurance that the basic principle of parental authority exercised in direct responsibility to God is solidly rooted in Scripture. With that confidence, fears of "overparenting," of "contaminating" interaction with rules and values, or of using "power" over our children, can be set aside.[2] Authority is vested in parents by God; and it is to God that we are responsible for the way in which we exercise that authority.[3] We are not locked in a power struggle with our children, but together with our children we live out roles and relationships prescribed by our Creator.

The second main source of confidence is in self-acceptance. If you think about people who are confident enough to lead, confident enough to exercise their gifts for God, confident enough to have opinions and convictions of their own, confident enough to dare to enjoy their children and live without constant fear—the word *self-worth* will probably pop into your mind. They are people who value themselves. Now this tends to be a tricky matter to discuss in Christian circles. Not so in secular ones, where *I'm OK—You're OK* has become the password, and contemporary psychology has been seeking ways of enhancing self-worth in the individual. But in conservative Christian circles there is some alarm at the use of words such as *self-worth* or even *self-confidence.*

"Self" is utterly suspect and to be put to the sword, or the cross, we are told. We run into a semantic problem unless we carefully clarify our terms. What is the construct "self" that such writers as Watchman Nee have warned us against so earnestly? [4] Surely it cannot mean the personality, or the essential, unique blend of gifts and abilities and handicaps and inabilities that makes each of us a distinct person. If that were so, we would be talking psychological suicide. And we would be speaking against our Creator who has made each of us for His honor and glory. We cannot exterminate our individuality without doing damage to something very special in the eyes of God.

We would be less confused if we talked about "death to selfishness" in its broadest sense: "me firstness" and "my wayishness" are the elements of the Adamic nature which are so troublesome that we must die to their influence in our actions and decisions. But "self" as identity, or uniqueness, or personhood, is something sacred.

Repeatedly in Scripture comes the assurance that God knows individuals from conception, that He knows people by name, that He is concerned and interested in every aspect of our development, and orders our circumstances to develop in us those traits which He can use for His purposes.[5]

If we are to be confident people, we must accept the fact that in God's eyes we are not only loved but of infinite worth as well. God has "crowned [man] with glory and honour" (Psalms 8:5 KJV). Ultimately, self-worth comes from a full revelation of the meaning of the death of the Lord Jesus Christ. As we read and reread the testimony of Scripture we come, one day, to the realization that Christ's death was for each of us as individuals, not just for humanity as a whole. Then we can join in the awe expressed by Isaac Watts:

> Alas! and did my Saviour bleed?
> And did my Sovereign die?
> Would He devote that sacred head
> For such a worm as I?

And in that moment of self-revelation when we recognize our own sinfulness as the reason for our Lord's death, we also find the wonder of self-acceptance. God Himself found me worthy of this incredible sacrifice. To Him I am not a "worm"! To Him I am of inestimable worth. Who am I to contradict His evaluation? And when I make this wonderful discovery, it takes me right out of the sphere of worrying about myself at all, for I am not loved because I am worthy; I am of infinite worth because I am loved.[6] In this confidence we are free to give ourselves in service. No longer do we need to mumble, "Ask someone else. I can't." Now, we say, "Because He died and rose again for me, I can!"

The third great source of confidence is the assurance of the indwelling Christ. Self-confidence is expressed in its Christian form in Paul's words: "I can do all things through Christ which strengtheneth me" (Philippians 4:13 KJV). There it is. This kind of confidence is the exact opposite of pride. It is not saying, "Look how great I am." It is not saying anything about oneself at all. It is simply acknowledging that the resources necessary to accomplish the tasks given us by God are available through God. "Not that we are sufficient of ourselves to think any thing as of ourselves; but our sufficiency is of God" (2 Corinthians 3:5 KJV).

I was signing books one night after a meeting at which I had spoken. People were chatting with me as I autographed, and I glanced up to see a dear friend in whose home Cam had once boarded. "Maxine," Alwyn said, with just a hint of a Welsh accent. "Here's a verse for you to speak on sometime: 'Christ in you, the hope of glory' " (Colossians 1:27 NAS). Recent illness had aged our friend but his deeply lined face shone with the glory of the truth that he whispered to me. "Isn't that what it's all about?"

How right he was. Here is the source of true confidence: Christ in me! How dare I feel unworthy, useless, insignificant? Christ in me! How dare I feel incompetent, ill equipped, unable? Christ in me! The power for present responsibilities and the hope of glory in the future.

For the parent who has trusted Jesus Christ as Saviour and committed his life to His Lordship, here is the source of real confidence. Pride is canceled out, as we recognize what Paul says pointedly: ". . . What do you have that you did not receive?" (1 Corinthians 4:7 NAS). A right view of the hand of God in our lives precludes arrogance. Whatever we have, He has given. Whatever our worth, it resides in His estimation. Whatever gifts or talents we may have, He has bestowed. Whatever we accomplish of any significance, He must do through us. "For without me ye can do nothing" (John 15:5 KJV).

And just as surely as this principle cancels out arrogance, so it cancels out self-abasement, that inverted form of pride that renders so many useless. It puts us in the sane, scriptural position which Paul urged the Romans to find: "Think your way to a sober estimate based on the measure of faith that God has dealt to each of you" (Romans 12:3 NEW ENGLISH BIBLE). It keeps us from thinking we are either more or less able than we are. And it keeps us in a dependent relationship with our God.

If we are to help our children to confidence, we as parents need to be confident. Confident that the Word of God is a true and sufficient guide. Confident that we are of immeasurable personal worth. Confident that, through the power of the indwelling Christ, we can do all things—including being parents.

We can answer the challenges hurled at us simply and sanely:

"We have been entrusted with children. With God's Word as our guide, we will exercise the authority of parenthood, acknowledging our responsibility to God for the carrying out of our tasks. Accepting ourselves and our children as His creations, we can function confidently, living under the power of the indwelling Christ. Of course we can cope with our kids!"

3

Kids Are Great!

The healthiest view of children is to see them as "people in process."

My oldest child was five, my youngest a tiny baby, when I chatted with Elenore, the mother of seven chilren. "Our oldest kids are teens now," she said, "and we are enjoying them so much. They are such wonderful friends. You know, we find it hard to break up after our supper hour, we're having such good conversation! The best times are all ahead, Maxine."

The baby days were great days. What could be more beautiful than a little child's soft hands clinging to your neck? The toddler days were exciting as the children experimented with language forms, learned skills, and began to operate as individuals displaying their own personalities. The middle-childhood days are also exciting. Our children move toward more sophisticated skills in a whole range of areas: they are real friends, and real companions, and we enjoy them very much. And this mother has told me that the best days are still ahead!

The concept of children as troublesome, expensive, and hard to handle creates pervasive anxiety in our society. Some young couples just decide not to have children at all. "If a family is that much trouble," they are saying, "then let's skip it." I want to say unequivocally: Kids are great. They are exciting. Their potential is simply phenomenal. And in any given family there is the potential to change this world for God.

If we are to have this kind of confidence as we look at our children, we will have to learn to see them from a perspective other than our own. From our own selfish viewpoint, children may be a nuisance, an expense, an unnecessary bother. But from God's point of view—as expressed to us in Scripture—children

are a gift and a reward (Psalms 127:3–5). Here are some fundamental perceptions about children which can help us—and
them—to confidence.

Perception #1. The perception of *individual worth* and *potential* is
fundamental. We understand the worth and potential of our children as we see them as individual human beings stamped with the
very image of God. This recognition of worth is reflected in the
way that successful parents interact with their children. Parents
who are successful with their children are parents who treat their
children with courtesy and respect. I have increasingly become
aware of the way in which people talk to children. I see people
ignore their children; shush children unnecessarily; speak to children rudely and harshly. But the people whom I most respect as
parents are those who talk to their children as they do to other
people: in tones of normal courtesy, in tones of friendship, of
acceptance. They are people who project by their voice and their
actions the message to the child, "You are okay. I like you." Of
course children are in need of chastisement sometimes; in need of
correction; in need of much training. But this should never
legitimize a rude or domineering or hostile attitude or tone of
voice.

The courtesy one extends to a child should rule out exercising
corporal disciplinary measures in front of others after a child is
three or so. It should include a firm and fair tone of voice, rather
than bossy nagging. We cannot hope for our theologians to teach
our children that they are of worth in God's eyes if we have not
communicated by our tone of voice, by our method of handling,
by our quiet, firm, consistent kindness, that we appreciate our
children and that they are indeed worthwhile people.

Perception #2. A second perception that we need to have is that
children are interesting. The idea that being home with children is
essentially a boring thing and that the real excitement lies out in a
laboratory, or classroom, or legal office, is a foolish fiction being
foisted on us today. The fact is that there is perhaps nothing as
interesting as a child's developing abilities, a child's awakening
understandings, a child's use of language. While we don't expect
the young child to contribute in a political or a theological discus-

sion, we need to quiet our hearts to hear what the child is telling us about God, about the world, about the way he's seeing things.

Not long ago, Mitchell and I were driving down a gravel road, Mitchell leaning over the front seat in his usual position, asking questions—his usual pastime. "Mom," he said, "are there walls between the earth and the sky?"

I was startled. We had a globe in our home, and I thought all the children knew that the earth was a ball.

"No, Mitchell." I replied. "It's not like that at all, honey. The earth is a big ball. It's so big that it looks flat, but really it's a big, round, huge ball. We're on the ball, and the sky is wrapped around the ball like a big blanket."

There was a long minute of quiet as spring calves and their mothers, flapping crows, and timorous gophers slid past our view. And then, suddenly, Mitchell exclaimed, "I get it! I get it now! We're *on* the ball, not *in* the ball!"

What fun to be with a child at the moment he reinterpreted his whole cosmology. I refuse the idea of children as boring. I certainly have not found them so. Of course there have been times when I was lonely for adult conversation, and always I was glad for the stimulation of good books. But as a mother who spent a lot of time with no company but that of my children, I can say that children are delightful and interesting people.

Perception #3. A third perception that we need to have concerning children is that *children are vastly more understanding than usually given credit for by their parents.* The fact is that the parent who observes carefully will discover that children, well before they are speaking, are grasping in very large measure the components of their world. They know when their parent is going to insist on obedience and when they can "get away with it." The knowledgeability of children is almost terrifying, except when viewed as the great gift that it is. To underestimate it is to talk down to children and limit their ability to maximize this potential. And so, whether you're looking at a two-month-old child, or a two-year-old child, or a ten-year-old child, I suggest you take what you think he knows and multiply it by ten to allow for that knowledgeability which comes by intuition, by pure absorption, and by endless observation.

Perception #4. When we deal with children in family, another perception we need to focus on is *individual differences*. While brothers and sisters may be seen as similar by onlookers, parents need to be aware of how unique each child is. A method for training or correcting one child is not necessarily the right one for another child. And it is the unique gifts and abilities of each child, his unique way of seeing and responding, that makes him such a gift to his family—and to the world.

One young family with which I visited told me about a plan they had for confirming and acknowledging the individuality of each member of the family. Once in a while, a week is specially designated and one member of the family is honored on each day. On "Peter Day," for instance, Peter is given a place of honor at the table, and during the supper hour, each member of the family tells something they appreciate about Peter. "The glow that this generates is really special," his mother told me.

Perception #5. As we look at children and marvel at their potential and their beauty, at the fact that we are again looking at a human being, in whom is the breath of life, and upon whom is the stamp of the very image of God, we have to perceive also *the effects of the Fall.* If we are honest, we know that we have not borne cherubs into the world. The natural tendency in children toward disobedience, defiance, and rebellion is a stark and saddening reality. And thus, even in early months, as we cope with our children we are coping with that basic dilemma of the human race: enormous potential for good and equally huge potential for evil locked into each and every individual. As we recognize the damage done to humanity by the Fall, we become aware of the need of our children for chastisement, correction, and training (*compare* Genesis 3 with Romans 5). And we realize that ultimately, their need is for regeneration—for that renewing of the image of God upon them that will attend their own personal acceptance of Jesus Christ as Saviour and Lord (Titus 3:5–7; 2 Corinthians 5:17).

Aware that our children need not just civilization but also salvation, we will nonetheless train and teach them. A patient woodsman lays everything in place in preparation for the striking of the match. And Christian parents will do everything they can to help their children so order their lives that when the fire of God does fall upon their lives, there will be a lifelong burning.

Perhaps the healthiest view of children is to see them as "people in process." *People:* individually loved and cared and planned for by their Father in heaven. But also *in process:* moving toward the realization of their full potential, and therefore in need of a period of dependency, a period of loving training under the authority of their parents. "Lo, children are an heritage of the Lord," the Psalmist says (Psalms 127:3 KJV). A good heritage. An exciting heritage. A heritage of immeasurable worth.

Seeing children as they are seen in the Word of God helps us to perceive their worth, their potential, their individuality, and their need of parental authority—all from a higher-than-human point of view.

4

Confidence and Self-Acceptance

Loving acceptance, both demonstrated and spoken, can lay the foundation for trusting confidence, and lead to self-acceptance.

Narrating a television documentary about L'Arche, a community of caring for retarded adults, Malcolm Muggeridge sat for a few quiet moments in the chapel there. "It was here I heard prayed a most memorable prayer," he said. "A retarded adult, who had known a lifetime of personal rejection, knelt just over there and prayed, 'God who made me as I am, help me accept myself as I am.'"

That prayer from L'Arche is a prayer we all need to learn to pray ourselves. And it is a prayer we need to help our children become able to pray as well.

Long before the child begins to see himself as an identity separate from others, the basis for acceptance of that identity is laid in parental acceptance. The sense that "I am loved *as I am*" is absolutely essential to confidence. From the earliest moment that the child is held, appreciation and acceptance can be shown and expressed. The mother who says, "Another boy? Oh, no!" expresses an underlying nonacceptance that may be felt by the child. Acceptance from the moment of birth can be accomplished if parents have prayerfully prepared their own hearts to accept that child as he or she is given to them.

I remember when one of our children was born. After several sessions of false labor and then many hours of final labor, she was born looking like a battered child: head misshapen, face bruised purple, eyes bloodshot. As the nurse showed her to me, compassion for my new daughter flowed through me. "It's been a tough trip, sweetheart," I murmured to her. "But you've made it. And you'll look better in the morning." We must accept our children, not as the advertiser's dream we may have pictured, but as they are—from the very moment of birth.

I read a book—the title and author of which I have forgotten—before the birth of our first child, which emphasized the need for verbal communication of love and acceptance to even the tiniest babies. So, from their earliest days, I talked and sang to the children. Often I improvised little songs or rhymes; sometimes I just talked to them. But the recurring theme, however it was worded, was simply acceptance.

"What a beautiful little person you are."

"I'm glad God chose us to be your parents. I'm glad God let you be born into our family. You are so very special."

"God made you so marvelously. I just thank Him for giving you to me to love."

I told them of our love for them and of God's love for them. And the chidren grew snug and secure within the knowledge of such love and acceptance. Erik Erikson characterizes the first of a series of identity-forming crises as the establishment of trust in early infancy.[7]

This, of course, requires more than mere talk. Trust—and its concomitant "virtue" of hope—

> relies for its beginnings on the new being's first encounter with
> *trustworthy maternal persons*, who respond to his need for *intake*
> and *contact* with warm and calming envelopment and provide food
> both pleasurable to ingest and easy to digest, and who prevent ex-
> perience of the kind which may regularly bring too little too late.[8]

But trust once placed in parents can be directed to One more trustworthy: ". . . the Father of all lights, with whom there is never the slightest variation or shadow of inconsistency" (James 1:17 J. B. PHILLIPS).

Loving acceptance, both demonstrated and spoken, can thus lay the foundation for trusting confidence, and lead to self-acceptance (or "autonomy" in Erikson's scheme of development).

The feedback from children comes early. Soon after Geoffrey could talk, he looked up one night from his supper with a happy smile. "You like Geoff?" he asked, obviously confident of a positive response. "Jesus like Geoff?" He waited happily for our reply, "Yes, He surely does."

A waitress in a restaurant chatted with Cammie, who was just over two. "Where did you get your blue eyes, sweetie?"

Without a moment's hesitation, Cammie replied, "From Jesus." Accepting themselves physically as God's handiwork is an important foundation for full personal acceptance.

"I will praise thee; for I am fearfully and wonderfully made" (Psalms 139:14 KJV), is a natural statement of praise in families where the goodness of God in creating the body is emphasized. A very early memory takes me back to a chilly frame house in a tiny Saskatchewan village. There, with water drawn from a central village well, bath time was a Saturday-night ritual conducted in the kitchen. At ages two and four, my little sister and I were washed in the square galvanized laundry tub by my mother, and briskly toweled by my father. I can still remember the warm glow of love filling the little kitchen, and the verbalization of their feelings: "Hasn't the Lord given the children beautiful bodies." There is no way of estimating the significance of such expression of appreciation and praise in the development of grateful self-acceptance.

Let's face it—people who cannot learn to accept and like their bodies find it very hard to really accept and like themselves. Our children need to appreciate, be aware of, and exult in the beauty and flexibility and strength of their growing bodies. Growth, of course, is an exciting element of body awareness. Growth charts against the wall; the fun of trying on last year's clothes; looking at tiny baby clothes now outgrown: all of these help the child relate positively to himself—his growing, changing self.

John Calvin called the body "a factory where innumerable operations of God are carried on," and suggests that a proper appreciation of the human body should cause people to "burst forth in His praise." In very early childhood, happy bath-time experiences with parental appreciation and the always-favorite game of "naming the parts" lays a foundation for this kind of praise. Later, as the child asks questions about various bodily functions, careful teaching should be given, with credit ascribed to God for His marvelous design. For, to quote Calvin again, ". . . the human race [is] a bright mirror of the Creator's works." [9] A good book with simple diagrams of the various body systems—digestive system, nervous system, respiratory system, circulatory system—is helpful in teaching these basics to preschoolers. We have one with simple transparent overlays that has become positively dog-eared from use.

Involved in bodily and personal acceptance is early acceptance of sex differences. Where there are brothers and sisters of similar age in a family, there is an early understanding of physiological differences. Where siblings are of one sex, friends or cousins to bathe with, or visiting babies being diapered, may offer the necessary visual explanation.

It is completely natural and normal that little children will explore all of their own body parts with a frank and innocent interest. Parents should not feel alarm or project anxiety about this. At the same time, they can early teach the idea of "private parts"—of modesty; of dealing with private functions in relative privacy. Unfortunately, "modesty" and "shame" have been confused in modern writing. They are not, of course, the same thing. Modesty is based on an acceptance that some parts of the body are special and private. Teaching it helps preclude public performance of toilet habits or excessive self-fondling. And it helps the child's sense of worth, rather than hindering it, because the child recognizes the special, private nature of his genital area.

Actually, shame is much more likely to be felt by a child who is allowed to run naked. The human body needs—since the Fall—a covering. And while parents may chuckle at a child's apparently uninhibited nakedness, above two or three years of age a child is likely to feel embarrassment and shame over it.

This was driven home unforgettably to me as I sat in a waiting room with one of our daughters. Since the specialist was a urologist, preparation for examination had included removing panties. My little girl, under her carefully pinned gown, was a bit uptight. But she had not cried, since I had carefully explained the necessity of this examination. As we waited, a terrible screaming struggle began in a nearby dressing room. In a few moments, a mother carried in a sobbing and deeply distraught boy of about the same age as my daughter. She turned to me. "I don't know what's the matter with him," she said. "We let him go naked at the lake all the time. And he sees his father and me naked at home all the time. And now he's got an obsession with modesty. I just can't get him to take his clothes off."

We sat in the waiting room: a little girl who had been taught modesty was able to wait without shame; a little boy who had not been taught modesty was uncontrollably unhappy and ashamed.

While from the age of three on, children become aware—whether they are taught or not—that they have "private parts," exposure of which is embarrassing to themselves and to others, private exploration of genitals is likely to continue for some time. It should not be a cause for concern, unless the child becomes excessively interested in stroking and fondling himself, and withdraws himself from others for this purpose. If that happens, constructive alternatives should be offered: something satisfying to hold or feel given to the child at bedtime might help to broaden his sensory experiences. Exploring his own body is preliminary to accepting it. After having come to terms with their own contours, most children will lose interest in this kind of self-exploration and turn their interest elsewhere, unless parental alarm or anxiety drives them inward and arouses a curiosity at a deeper level.

Whether or not your child is a beauty, you can help him to accept and appreciate his appearance. Every child has some praiseworthy feature—beautiful eyes, perhaps. Or nice hands. Or a pretty smile. "Everything is beautiful in its own way" should be an early discovery. "You look so nice," is something a parent should say often to a child. Early attempts at his own grooming should be praised and encouraged. The individual human being must learn to live within the body and behind the face he has been given. Early acceptance of both is important to his self-acceptance.

A young woman shared with me, "My dad believed in being honest—scrupulously so. All the time I was growing up, he would say, 'You're such a scrawny little thing,' or 'The Lord certainly made you homely, honey.' I fight all the time against feelings of self-loathing. I may look neat and attractive—but I *feel* ugly most of the time." That's a tragedy. That kind of honesty is a cruel thing, as is all truth without love. Be honest with your children by finding "whatsoever things are lovely" and helping both the child and those around him to "think on these things" (Philippians 4:8 KJV). It is one of the important ways in which confidence is built.

Of course children will early notice some individual differences. A child with a disability or a disfigurement will have to be given additional reassurance, honest building of a positive self-image. In particular, it is important within a family to avoid comparison between children, or the setting up of competition for "praise points." The scriptural truth of the value of diversity is an important one to understand and communicate within a family.[10] "I'm glad you're *you,*" needs to be not only stated but also shown in equal attention, equal appreciation, and equal love for all of the children in a family.

In teaching our children self-acceptance, we have to make some moves to limit the inputs of nonacceptance during the very early, formative years before school. Thus, a grandparent who shows obvious favoritism, or who draws negative comparisons between one child and another, needs to be firmly told that this is unacceptable. We need to guard our own responses, both verbal and nonverbal, to our children. Put-downs such as, "Why are you such a sloppy kid?" should neither be said nor shown. Parents must learn to always speak respectfully of the child.

Not long ago I was at a social function. A four- or five-year-old boy came and sat quietly beside me. After an opener from me, he chatted merrily and very attractively with me. Later, I saw him with his mother. "Is this your little fellow?" I asked, indicating the child.

"Yes," she grimaced, "and sometimes I wish he weren't."

"Oh, never!" I couldn't restrain myself from protest. "He's a fine boy. You should be proud of him."

"Sometimes," she shrugged, and sailed on.

I cried in my heart for a little child with great potential, but with a ceiling put on his confidence development by a mother too insecure to be accepting, too worried about how he reflected on her own self-image to be supportive. Of course there are times when our children disappoint us, times when they embarrass us. But these do not have to be detailed to others. Your child should most often hear you speak warmly, acceptingly, and approvingly of him. From infancy, he will know by your tone your feeling for him.

Put-down teasing (and some psychologists say that all teasing has this effect) should not be a part of family routines.[11] A teased child most often defends himself by becoming smart-alecky or "lippy" in return—and who can blame him? If parents must tease, let them be sure to tease only in areas of the child's strength, areas in which the child feels secure enough to be able to laugh with the teasing. This security should not be overassumed: a child's identity and self-image is very fragile and highly dependent on feedback from those around him. I am not suggesting that a child should never be teased—but always lovingly, gently, and with a view to helping him learn how to respond to teasing. Since he is sure to be teased by his peers, parental teasing can help him learn techniques of self-defense. But parents should never use teasing as a way of pointing out the child's defects or weaknesses. Where correction is needed, let it be done straightforwardly, rather than by the devious method of put-down teasing.

One of the most constant and potentially most destructive types of negative input comes from brothers and sisters. To try to monitor all of sibling interaction is a task that is beyond even the most diligent parent. But one can be alert to trends. When jeering or teasing is often directed at one child by several other members of the family, it should be stopped. Children should not be allowed to belittle one another.

Most families have a pair of children who are classic sibling rivals: competitive and hostile. I don't know of any theory that really explains why this happens. Burton L. White hypothesizes that "the younger the older child is [when the sibling is born] the more aggravating and problematic . . . sibling relationships are." [12] He suggests that children should be spaced about three years apart to minimize sibling hostility and jealousy problems. My own observations do not particularly bear this out. In our own family, the first two children (spaced only seventeen months apart) are classic sibling rivals. But the younger two children, with only fifteen months between birthdays, have never exhibited rivalry. Other mothers have told me that their most serious intersibling problems are with those children who were spaced three years apart.

Obviously, there are no magic formulas—not even as to spacing of births—which will resolve the problems of sibling conflicts. The variables are just too many. Probably the personality types of the children involved is the most important factor. But it does help to remember that sibling rivalry is a natural part of family living. It is as old as the first family. But it need not have such disastrous results. Brothers and sisters should not be allowed to hurt each other physically or psychically. Siblings who have a hard time getting along with each other should be buffered from continuous contact: sent to do separate chores, given separate club or sports activities, perhaps. While accepting that the family is a personal-relations laboratory in which children learn how to cope with hostilities, teasing, and friendships on a day-to-day basis, you can consciously work toward minimizing the damage done to self-esteem by a continuous stream of negative inputs from a brother or sister.

(As a parent I take considerable consolation, however, from the fact that neither Joseph in the Old Testament nor Jesus in the New were seriously damaged by lack of sibling acceptance.)

The better job you do of helping your child to develop social skills—please-and-thank-yous, sharing of toys, nonaggressive play (no biting, pinching, or scratching allowed)—the better self-image your child will develop. This will be partly because he finds himself more acceptable to others, with a reduction in negative feedback, and partly because he will have more self-respect when he knows that he can control himself.

Firm and steady discipline coupled with love and acceptance tells the child that someone cares. Loving discipline is a mark of parental esteem, a proof that the child is considered worthy of correction and guidance. And this feeds into a sense of self-worth and hence of self-acceptance.

Children should not hear or overhear comments such as, "Kids are sure expensive these days." Their anxiety about causing financial problems for their parents can be painfully acute. Nor should they grow up hearing—or feeling—that "kids are a nuisance." Probably these statements will be put more subtly: "Well, if we didn't have three kids, we could go away this winter, too." However phrased, such statements should simply not be made.

In primitive societies, children were warmly accepted partly because they could assist with daily labor and help to create an economic base for the family unit.[13] In Western society today, children usually do not make an economic contribution. But they should nonetheless be assured that of all of life's treasures, they are the most precious to their parents.

Wise and considerate parents who keep their tongues under "the law of kindness" (Proverbs 31:26 KJV) can build into their chidren self-acceptance. And this self-acceptance forms the foundation for confidence—and ultimately, the ability to look life in the eye.

5

Confidence and Reassurance

Reassuring our children means helping to work through and overcome fears; to accept and learn from mistakes; to evaluate or dismiss hostile and negative inputs.

The young engineer who lunched with us was a leader in a local motorcycle club. He was close to kids—tough kids. He knew where they were at. He himself had consumed a good deal of his obviously exceptional brainpower in devising methods for escaping work and retribution while still in high school. Somehow, he had gotten through the courses, on to college, and now was practicing his profession. But he had his finger on the pulse of modern teenagers. And he was concerned. "There's something wrong," he mused. "Something missing from kids. It's something I call 'inner toughness.' And they don't have it. They're scared of life."

The "something" our friend called "inner toughness" is a steel cable of many strands including character and confidence. One of the ways we can foster the development of confidence is through reassurance which gradually becomes internalized by the child.

It is not only teens who are "scared of life." Little children spend much of their time being "scared to death," especially at night, when monsters lurk and nightmares torment. Night after night, when Heather Ruth was almost three, we would be awakened by the sudden pell-mell running of her feet up the stairs. She would have gone down the stairs quietly, moving toward the light that glowed in the bathroom. Now she would be returning to her little bunk niche.

"What the matter, Heather?" I would waken and call—often, I admit, impatiently.

"They didn't get me," she would reply.

"They?"

45

"The bears." Her voice was quavery. "On the stairs."

All children experience fearfulness: lions spring out of dream
TV sets to tear and devour; villainous faces from television cartoons and books return to haunt and harry; monsters lurk in the
corners of darkened rooms. And, however absurd the fears may
seem to the adult, they are very real and terrifying to the child.
Learning to cope with fearfulness is important if the child is to
develop confidence.

Where do all the monsters and all the nighttime terrors that
haunt children come from? Some can be directly traced, such as
images replayed from television. Yet that still leaves unanswered
the question of why little children are so morbidly fascinated by
the horrible. There is something in the monstrous that answers to
the child's unconscious awareness of evil within himself.[14] The
pain and bondage of these fears can be seen as a direct result of
the Fall. I have been impressed by the prevalence of the snake
image in terror-inducing dreams my children have wakened from.
It seems to me that children somehow inherit mankind's troubled
memory of Paradise Lost.

Many of the monsters are fears with faces. As adults, we name
our fears and thus identify them. We say, "I have claus-
trophobia," or "I can't stand heights." But children do not have
the words or the concepts with which to handle the great, dark
world of human fearfulness. And so they have monsters
instead—monsters that seldom materialize except at night. And
the more vivid the child's imagination, the greater the input into
his mind of bizarre or malicious faces of TV and comic books, the
more acute will be his dread as nighttime reactivates memories
and inflates them into full-sized terrors. It is partly because children do cope with monstrous fantasies, with frightening nightmares and terrifying imaginations, that those really horrible fairy
tales are so popular with children. In those stories, the monsters
or villains are clearly identifiable and they get what they deserve:
they get chopped up, decapitated, utterly destroyed. This is entirely different from the television serials in which the villains
linger to return week after week—and are only punished, never
destroyed. In the vengeance wreaked upon the evil giants and
trolls of fairy stories, children find some of their fears exorcised.[15]

Fearfulness in children is unavoidable—and it is not all negative. When it leads to proper reassurance, it can lead the child on toward confidence. But some measures can be taken to reduce the amount of fearfulness that troubles children. It is wise to limit the amount of "fearful intake." Much of what is called "children's programing" on television is in the form of cartoons that play up fear or cruelty as an element. Use the "off" button firmly to reduce the number of ugly or horrible faces that get implanted in your child's mind. Avoid having comic books—"Christian" or otherwise—for little tots to see. They tend to be ugly in their exaggeration of facial expressions and are potentially troubling to very young children.

Another preventive step for nighttime fearfulness is a reassuring sequence of bedtime rituals. A fun-filled bath-and-story time is sometimes more than a tired mother can muster, but it surely is ideal. Perhaps husband and wife can work out a system for sharing the duties of this highly important time of the day. Perhaps Dad can wrestle and roll with the children and then bathe and get them into pajamas while Mother tidies up the kitchen and gets the dishes done—or at least in soaking. Then the family can sit down together for a quieter phase: story time, a song, a good-night prayer together.

Wrapped in his parents' love, clean and tired, a little one can be tucked into bed and expected to go to sleep. It is well not to darken the child's room entirely: leave a door a bit ajar so that the hall light glows in; or have a tiny night-light to plug into the wall. Now, with the little one in bed, you can stand by the bedside for a few moments and talk softly and reassuringly. "Jesus has promised to be with us always, in the nighttime as well as in the daytime." Speak positively of the dark, quiet night. "God sends us nighttime so we can sleep and get ready for another day. What a good plan. I'm so thankful for bedtime." (And *that* is sure to be a true statement from a mother tucking preschoolers into bed!)

I'm no soloist, but the children used to love to have me sing for them as they snuggled into their beds. We had a favorite good-night song which assured them, "My God is watching o'er you, His presence goes before you." Apart from the time that one of the children called me back to ask when he could open "God's presents," that song seemed to be a good, reassuring closer.

A favorite doll or toy to tuck in alongside the child is another kind of reassurance. One particularly pleasant good-night toy we were given was a Raggedy Ann doll with a built-in music box that played "Brahms' Lullaby" when the cord was pulled. An occasional after-lights-out visit from Mother or Dad helps children to feel positive and happy about bedtime, too.

Preschoolers, even after having settled peacefully for the night, are often awakened by nightmares. It can save you from getting up several times a night if you have an open-door policy on your own room after you have settled for the night. A little one can feel free to come to your bedside, talk to you, or climb in for a short time of hugging and reassuring. Remember that vivid dream images may linger in technicolor for several minutes after a dream has been broken off. During that time, let the child talk about the dream, then gradually divert his attention to happier things. "Let's list five of our favorite things . . . ." "Let's talk about how Jesus stilled the storm . . . ." Gradually center your child's attention on the power and presence of Jesus Christ, helping him to develop positive patterns of thought. A prayer together can go a long way toward emptying a child's mind of difficult images and reassuring him of God's presence.

Children are, of course, incredibly knowing. A child who finds that his parents respond to his fearfulness may come down night after night whispering, "I'm afraid." And your thoughtful reassurance may serve to reinforce a behavior pattern which is disruptive both to you and to the child. You will have to be prayerful and careful in discerning when this game is being played. Firmly but briefly reassure the child and send him back to his own room with the words, "I don't want you to get up again tonight."

Of course, nighttime fearfulness is not the only kind of fear for which a child may need reassurance. Children are often afraid of having their parents leave. Psychologists tell us that the greatest childhood fear is the fear of losing one's parents, called "separation anxiety." And so the clinging of a child whose parents are going out for the evening is quite understandable. A regular baby-sitter who really takes time to read to the child and play with him can make such partings much easier. Wouldn't *you* be afraid to be left with a stranger? On the first visit with your children, the baby-sitter should have some time with the children while you are still at home, to familiarize both sitter and child with each other. Then, a firm and loving good-bye (ah! those sticky last kisses on your freshly made-up cheek) and a quick exit will help both sitter and child. Always remember that children are capable of a great deal of understanding. Tell them where you are going and when you are coming back. Fill the void of the unknown with reasonable explanations, and children will be reassured.

Many children have phobias of various kinds. Parents must remember that children differ dispositionally from each other. One may be very timid and easily frightened; another bold to the point of brassiness. The most timid of our four children was Heather Ruth, number three. Her fears were many: big machinery starting up; loud noises; thunderstorms; my leaving her. But worst of all, she was afraid of fire. And so a summer day when she was not quite five is especially memorable, for she was confronted by a direct challenge to that fear.

With the two girls, I was driving on a country road when we noticed that a neighbor's windbreak was aflame.

"Looks like maybe they were burning grass and the fire got away on them," I commented. "Guess we had better see if we can help." We drove toward the fire.

As we neared the yard, we could see that the fire was very much out of control: great orange flames crackled in the trees on three sides of the house. To our astonishment, we found no one at home. Now it was not a case of helping the neighbors fight their fire—but of dealing with it ourselves.

One row of flaming trees was within a few feet of the side of the house. I hooked up the garden hose and set undauntable Cammie to work spraying them. Heather Ruth, choking and crying with both smoke and terror, cringed inside the car. But now I had to back our car out of the yard—and I needed Heather Ruth to come to the house with me. "I need your help, Heather. I'll look after you. You won't get hurt, honey. Just come and do what I tell you." Trembling and crying, torn between fear and trust, she obeyed. As I phoned other neighbors and the village fire department, Heather Ruth pluckily stood on a stool at the sink and began filling pails with water. I ran in and out of the house, a one-woman bucket brigade, calling encouragement to Heather Ruth. She never did manage to stop the tears, until neighbors arrived with more hoses and gradually other hands took over the work.

But when the fire was over, fearful little Heather Ruth shared in the praise that was given to two little girls who had fought fire together. The story became one she delighted to tell. About two months later, she fought her fear again and stood with me to watch a demolition bonfire at our new house site. This time, she found herself able to really look at the fire. "Look at the flames running up the board—just like little mice," she whispered. At last she could not only cope with her fear but also relate positively and confidently to fire.

Children also need reassurance when they have made mistakes or had accidents. An accident is not a crime. A mistake is—at least usually—not a catastrophe. The child must face the consequences of a mistake or accident: he can help wipe up the spill; he can experience a week without his bike because it needs repairs. He can be taught the seriousness of the possible danger to himself or others caused by his heedlessness. He may need to be punished for disobedience that has resulted in problems. But he needs to be reassured that he is not stupid, that everybody in the world makes mistakes, and that erring is part of the human condition.

As children venture out, away from home, into the playground and school situation, they will experience hostile and negative inputs. Particularly if the child represents an ethnic or racial minority, if he has a disability or disfigurement, or if his speech or clothing or behavior are significantly different from other children's, he will be the object of various kinds of scorn. No child is immune from this—except perhaps the bully who sets other children's prejudices into action. Again, the child needs parental reassurance that it is okay to be different. Children need to be helped to an intelligent self-acceptance so that they can cope with negative inputs—far more than they need parents who angrily phone neighbors or school principals to "set things straight." A child who has been enveloped in acceptance in his early years will have a foundational self-respect which can keep him from despair in the face of taunts and teasing which children fling at each other. Nonetheless, he will need frequent reassuring as he goes through these experiences.

Reassuring our children means more than comforting them. It means helping to work through and overcome fears; to accept and learn from mistakes; to evaluate or dismiss hostile and negative inputs. All of these are parental tasks in helping children toward confidence. The result is "inner toughness"—the kind of courage that enables people to live by their convictions, to do what they have to do in life. This kind of courage is not the absence of fear. It is going ahead with life despite the fear. It is the kind of inner toughness that took Shadrach, Meshach, and Abednego *to* the fiery furnace: God Himself brought them *through* it (Daniel 3). This is the kind of confidence our children will need if they are to live for God. Let's build it into them through reassurance and challenge.

6

Confidence and Competence

Each competence that is mastered by the child contributes to an overall feeling of "I can"—a most important element in any positive approach to life.

"I used to think you were awfully hard on your kids," Joy confided. "But you know something? I think it's good for them!"

We talked about the interdependence of competence and confidence, about parents taking time to teach their children how to achieve their high expectations. "The child who *can't* is one who lacks confidence," I said. "And he's usually just a child whose parents have not taken the time to give him competence training. The child who *can*—in a whole range of things—feels good about himself."

A few days later, we talked again. "Hey!" Joy said, "I've just lived through an example of what we were talking about. The other day I told Johnny to clean up his room. I mean, really clean it up. I didn't let him quit until the job was done. And afterward, he was so proud. He said, 'I really can help you, can't I, Mum? You know something? I like myself today.' "

Joy's experience certainly checked out against mine. A sense of competence is essential to a healthy self-image. Everything a child can do and do well contributes to a positive sense of self-worth, and the confidence that comes from independence. Parents can help their children achieve confidence by means of a cycle of activities I call the "Competence-Confidence Cycle" (Figure 1).

Each competence that is mastered by the child contributes to an overall feeling of "I *can*"—a most important element in any positive approach to life. A friend of mine who is responsible for hiring teachers for a large city school system tells me that over and over again he encounters young people who lack nothing except this all-important feeling of confidence. "They're well

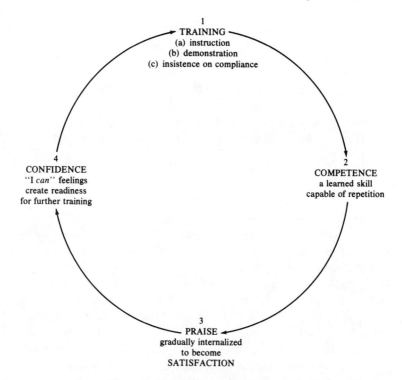

Figure 1. Competence-Confidence Cycle.

educated and bright," he tells me. "But they lack the assurance that they can handle the classroom tasks. So they're beaten before they start."

We had a little homemade ditty, a jingle we sang when zippers stuck or projects got tough:

> I can do it, I can do it, if I really try.
> When it's hard I just try harder—
> Never helps to fuss and cry.
> When it's hard I just try harder,
> Try and try and try and try.

There was a triumphant chorus for singing when the task was done:

Look, Mom, I did it,
I did it by myself.
I did it! I did it!
I did it all by myself.

There are three areas of basic competence in which children can develop in the preschool years: personal-care skills; helping skills; and survival skills. All can be taught by the method shown on the "Competence-Confidence Cycle" at the relevant stage of the child's development. Let's look at each of these areas.

1. Personal-care skills. Between the first and second year, children learn how to feed themselves and usually make a start on the toilet-training process. By the time the child is three, he is at that delightful stage: walking, talking, and toilet trained! The relief a mother feels in getting a little one to this stage is matched only by the pride and independence of the young one who has reached that stage. Erikson characterizes this as the achieving of autonomy; the freedom from utter dependence on others.[16]

All the ins and outs of teaching children how to eat and excrete have been endlessly detailed. There are probably as many ways to accomplish the ends as there are mother-child pairings. Probably the best conclusion that can be drawn from all the contradictory material on the subject is that you should start when you are ready and quit when you are done. Throw away the rule books and do what works for you and your child.

Teaching a child to feed himself can proceed from finger foods to spoon handling as the child is ready to cope. If you can stand the mess, let the child play with his food. If you can't—don't. Nothing will be gained by your being tolerant because some psychologist tells you you must be, if you find yourself fighting down a churning stomach.

Firm, loving toilet training, with warm, positive reinforcement in praise or immediate reward (such as a little candy) for compliance can be carried on during the child's second year, if the mother has patience. Or it can be left till later, if the mother has even more patience.

Other basic personal skills include dressing, bathing, and, later, grooming. These can be taught progressively from about the second birthday on. Dressing is a very important learning activity, involving eye-hand coordination, matching skills (socks go on feet, mittens on hands), and manipulative skills. By the time a child is three or so, he can be invited to select his own clothing within a designated range of choices. For example, he could select from three or four pairs of play pants in a drawer, and then be invited to choose a coordinating shirt and socks. The exercise of choice is an important step in developing independence and confidence.

Bathing is a favorite fun time for children. Children above two years of age can be left to play in a bathtub, as long as the door is open and a parent is on the alert. It's a happy way to conclude a day's play, with the cleaning process incidental to water play. Children can play at swimming lessons, tea parties, hairdressing, and an endless number of other games, while bathing—especially if there are two to play together. Empty plastic cups and bottles invite pouring (and pouring liquid from one container into another can help children toward developing important concepts such as volume); washable soap crayons can be used for drawing masks and body designs; soaped hair can be piled and sculpted into marvelous hairdos; bubbles and suds are endlessly fascinating. By the time the child is four, he can be taught how to wash himself systematically. In one more area, a skill which he learns can relieve the workload for parents and contribute to the child's self-esteem.

An interest in grooming can be encouraged by the availability of good mirrors at a height at which children can easily see. The mirror reflection is important in helping a child see himself as others see him. We put inexpensive full-length mirrors on the inside of each bedroom door. For dressing up, parading, making faces—and ultimately, for grooming—the children have made good use of the mirrors.

2. Helping skills. Long gone is the idea that the mother's main role is to pick up after the children. From the age of two, children can be taught to pick up their toys. Progressively after that they can learn other "tidiness" skills: tidying up their rooms; making their beds; putting clean clothes into drawers and dirty ones into hampers; scrubbing out the bathtub after a bath.

By the time they are five, children are often eager to help with routine cleaning tasks. This satisfies their need for meaningful accomplishment, for making a real contribution to family life. They can run a vacuum cleaner—although you may have to finish up edges and corners. They can whisk down a set of stairs, or even damp-sponge an area of the floor. They can dust furniture and dry dishes. And these are tasks that children of four and five really delight in, because they can participate in "real grown-up work."

The wise parent will cash in on the child's time of interest, for when the child says, "Can I help you?" training is most efficient. Of course it takes time to show a child how to do the task. But it is time well spent. It is an investment in your child's development of confidence.

And, of course, with helping skills there are lots of educational side effects that are beneficial. Drying cutlery and sorting it by pattern, then putting away knives and forks and spoons in their places, teaches a child rather sophisticated matching skills. Counting and arithmetic games are a natural when working with dishes. "How many plates are there in the pan? Let's count." Or, "How many forks have you dried? Count them while you put them away." Setting a table can be taught by the time the child is five—and with this task, the child can learn to tell left hand from right hand. Perhaps the most important educational by-product is that the child learns to follow directions and to carry out operations that consist of several steps in a fixed sequence: all foundational to further educational experience.

I found it useful to train my children to answer the telephone. "I can always tell when we've gotten through to your place," an American publisher told me. "We get your kids with their cute little Canadian accents." After the age of four, children can be taught to answer the phone, speaking clearly and courteously. Later, they can learn how to take and record messages as well.

3. Survival skills. This is a group of skills which are essential to a child's survival in the event of an emergency. Telephone skills are important here, too. From the age of three or four, the child should be taught how to dial "O" for emergency help. By the time he is four, the child should know his own telephone number, family name, and address. These can be taught by simple rote memorization. By the time he is five, the child should know by heart, or at least know exactly how to find, the telephone numbers of several adults living nearby who could be contacted if help were needed.

Teaching a child how to make a simple meal: a peanut-butter sandwich and a glass of milk, or—when he is five or so—how to open and heat a can of soup, gives him another basic survival skill. Training children on routes for swift and safe evacuation of the house is also important—and a proven lifesaver.

In our industrialized society, our children have been cut off from meaningful participation in the adult world. In more primitive societies, children were taught basic adult skills from an early age, largely by just being with adults who were engaged in growing or hunting food, preparing food, or making garments. Now, most adult activities are too technologically sophisticated for children to engage in, and take place far from the child's world. The home, however, can be a workshop in which children can participate in a wide range of activities which are not only interesting but real as well. This meets a child's need to be a functioning part of his society; it satisfies his *"sense of industry."* [17]

Domestic skills are helpful to the parent and easily accessible to the child. However, perceptive parents can teach many other competencies as well. Simple carpentry, sewing, basic mechanical skills, gardening: these and numerous other skills can be taught to children, at least in rudimentary form, from a very early age.

Competence does bring about confidence, and it is in that confidence that children can become contributing members of society. Parents who are hard on their kids, expecting a good level of performance from them and offering the training necessary to meet those expectations, will have kids who make a contribution to family life, and kids who feel confident that, with experience and training, they *can do*—whatever needs to be done.

7

The Ultimate Confidence

Conversion by faith in Jesus Christ is the ultimate confidence.

A childhood memory floats back . . . .

There was a tumult of joy in the backseat of our family car. My parents turned to find out what the excitement was about—to learn that my brother and I had just led my four-year-old sister to receive Christ as her Saviour.

"For the third time," my sister Marg remembers wryly.

Such evangelistic fervor may not be uncommon among children in evangelical homes. But it is the parents who bear the burden of responsibility. Christian parents are concerned about when and how little children can come to have "saving faith."

Maryanne, a dear friend with a very young family, expressed her concern to me. "We got a letter the other day from some friends," she said. "In it, they reported that all their children— aged three, five, and seven, had received Christ as Saviour. Is it possible for salvation to be meaningful at such an early age?"

There could hardly be a more important question for Christian parents to ask, for conversion by faith in Jesus Christ is the ultimate confidence—for children and for their parents; for this life and the next.

Knowing that he is accepted as a son in God's family (John 1:12), the child can enter into the fullest measure of self-acceptance. Knowing that his sins are forgiven (1 John 1:9; Acts 10:43), he becomes able to forgive himself for his own shortcomings. The assurance of eternal life (John 10:27, 28) can banish the haunting fear of death and separation. And, as he is made aware of the power of the indwelling Christ, the child can live in the quiet confidence that, "I can do all things through Christ which strengtheneth me'' (Philippians 4:13 KJV).

For his weakness and inabilities, the child can find Christ's strength (2 Corinthians 12:9, 10). For his sin, Christ's sacrifice (1 Peter 1:18, 19). For his fears, Christ's presence—always (Hebrews 13:5, 6; Matthew 28:20). For his feelings of inadequacy and self-rejection, he can find Christ's acceptance and love (Ephesians 1:3–7).

But how do we help preschoolers toward knowing this ultimate confidence? It is obvious that few preschoolers will experience ''conversion'' in the dramatic ''Saul of Tarsus'' mode (Acts 9). But they can take a first step on the Christian pilgrimage by personally opening their lives to Jesus Christ. And the Christian parent can help them to develop concepts preparatory to this at a very early age.

Let's clarify something right here: The limits of a child's understanding need not be the limits of his faith. Nobody ever *fully* understands the miracle of God's grace in a person's life. Even the most articulate analyst—a John Calvin or a Jonathan Edwards—cannot state exactly *how* God saves a trusting person. ''The wind blows where it likes,'' Jesus said. ''You can hear the sound of it but you have no idea where it comes from and where it goes. Nor can you tell how a man is born by the wind of the Spirit'' (John 3:8 J. B. PHILLIPS). I do not know just *how* Christ's death atoned for my sins, but God's Word says that it did—and I exercise saving faith by believing that Word (1 Peter 2:24; Romans 5:6–11).

So the limitations of children's concepts concerning God and sin and salvation need not be a stumbling-block to their receiving Christ into their lives. They can grow into knowledge as they develop and mature in their faith, just as all Christians need to ''grow in grace, and in the knowledge of our Lord and Saviour Jesus Christ'' (2 Peter 3:18 KJV).

What, then, must a child know in order to make an act of saving faith?

1. He must have a concept of God. God as Father, Creator, and Sovereign Lord: these are big concepts. Parent who pray with and for their children; who talk often with them about God, their loving Father; who tell about God's attributes of greatness and goodness in story, conversation, worship, and praise: these parents help children build a framework into which developing concepts can be placed.

The invisibility of God makes teaching about Him different from teaching about the material things in a child's environment. But the parent may have more trouble with this than does the child. To little children, things that are not seen are as real as things that do appear (Hebrews 11:1–6). A little child goes by faith in many areas of life—and as long as his basic trust is not disappointed, he has a resource of faith which is very deep.

"God is everywhere. He is a Spirit—so He does not have to be limited to being in one place at a time. Why, He is here with us right now! Let's talk with Him." The parent who lives in an awareness of the presence of God can introduce that Presence to the child at a very early stage.

Of course, parents have to be alert to correct misconceptions. Attempts by children to visualize God will usually result in the absurd: like Brian in W. O. Mitchell's *Who Has Seen the Wind* (Toronto: Macmillan), they may develop a little, manageable, pocket-sized God whom they can take out of their pockets and talk to from time to time, or a whiskery, genial, Santa Claus image—remote but benevolent.

Partial or incorrect concepts are best dealt with by patient explanation and continuous teaching. A child can't begin to assimilate a complete knowledge of God in a lesson or two. The "knowledge of the holy" (Proverbs 30:3 KJV) is a lifetime task for anyone. In daily conversation, in reading from the Scripture, in prayer, children will be exposed to their parents' God. And the God they come to know will be very much like the God of their parents. That's a sobering thought: parents might well do some mind stretching on their own concept of God. *Your God Is Too Small* by J. B. Phillips; *The Knowledge of the Holy* by A. W. Tozer; or J. I. Packer's *Knowing God* would help a serious adult to correct inadequacies in his knowledge of God.

For the human need to visualize God, He Himself has supplied the picture. The New International Version puts it: "For God who said, 'Let light shine out of darkness,' made his light shine in our hearts to give us the light of the knowledge of the glory of God in the *face of Christ* (2 Corinthians 4:6, *italics mine; compare* John 1:14–18). And so we tell our children—as God's Word tells us—that while nobody has ever seen God, we can visualize Him and relate to Him in the person of the Lord Jesus Christ.

2. He must have knowledge of the Lord Jesus Christ. In a home where Jesus Christ is honored as Lord in the lives of the parents, nothing could be more natural than to teach the little children about the person of Christ. The cycling calendar year, with its high points at Christmas and Easter, makes a natural framework into which to fit the stories of Christ's Incarnation, His life, His death, His Resurrection and Ascension. The stories of Jesus never cease to excite the wonder of little children. Tell them, read them from storybooks, read them from the Gospels, sing them— for if children are to exercise saving faith, they must first know of the Saviour.

Doctrinal elements are easily shared within the framework of the stories—shared in the same way that the writers of the Gospels share them. By pointing to the fulfillment of the Old Testament pictures and prophecies; by drawing conclusions from the "signs and wonders" Jesus performed (John 4:48 KJV); by listening to Jesus' own words—the Gospel writers, and we with them, acknowledge the full deity and the total humanity of Jesus Christ. "Jesus is the Son of God" is the simplest formulation for children. We can share with children that, though Jesus was once a child and experienced all the frustrations and temptations of childhood, He never sinned. And we can share with them that, as the sinless Son of God, He died in our place, taking the penalty of our sins, and rose again to live forever.

3. He must be aware of his own sinful self. The concept of "self" as separate from others is one which develops very early. The idea of "sin" is more easily understood by children than adults realize. Consider this comment by psychoanalyst Bruno Bettelheim:

> There is a widespread refusal to let children know that the source of much that goes wrong in life is due to our very own natures—the propensity of all men for acting aggressively, asocially, selfishly, out of anger and anxiety. Instead, we want our children to believe that,

inherently, all men are good. But children know that *they* are not always good; and often, even when they are, they would prefer not to be.[18]

Parents who avoid correcting a child or telling him that he has done wrong for fear of inflicting guilt are, quite simply, missing the point. Children are aware, deeply aware, of the sin nature within them, aware of the conflict between good and evil desires. They live with guilt—without any help from their parents. Forgiveness is as real a need to a child as it is to an adult.

With the concepts of God, self, and sin, and a knowledge of the person of Jesus Christ, a preschool child *may* be ready to receive Christ as Saviour for himself. The opportunity can be afforded at an appropriate time—after a child has shown genuine sorrow for his sin, or has expressed a deep love response to the Lord Jesus. "Would you like to ask Jesus to come into your life?" the parent could ask. If there is no pressure, children respond very honestly. "Not yet," a four-year-old might very well say. Or, "I will when I'm ready."

When a child does answer with a yes, the parent can lead him in a simple prayer, something such as this:

Dear Father,
   I know that I am a sinner. I am sorry that I have made You sad so often.
   I believe that Jesus, Your Son, died for me and rose again.
   Right now, I am asking the Lord Jesus to be my Saviour. Please forgive my sins and give me eternal life.

> In Jesus' name I pray.
> Thank You.
> Amen.

If the child hesitates, pause for further explanation. If his attention shifts, just let the matter drop until another time. When the child does make an act of acceptance and commitment, do not expect a radical transformation. Your parenting is not finished! Discipline, development, and patient teaching will all still have their part in your child's growth.

Andrew Murray wisely warns against making either too much
or too little of early-childhood profession of faith.

> We need to be kept from right-hand as well as left-hand errors. On
> the one side, we must beware of considering a child's religious im-
> pressions of little value. Like all beginnings of life and growth, they
> may be feeble and easily lost; they are still of infinite value as the
> preparation for that which abideth ever. We must, on the other side,
> be kept from overestimating or trusting in it. We must remember that
> the tender plant needs unceasing watching, and that only in the
> congenial atmosphere of a home holy to the Lord and wholly dedi-
> cated to His service can we count on its ripening fruit to eternal
> life.[19]

Or, as my mother puts it succinctly: "Childhood faith must mature to become saving faith."

In the Zuck and Getz study of Christian youth, it was found
that one out of eight Christian young people had received Christ
as Saviour before the age of six.[20] Of these, 92.2 percent came
from homes in which both parents were Christians. I can speak as
a representative of this large group of Christians with a preschool
salvation experience. I remember a clear act of receiving Christ
as Saviour when I was about five years old.

My preschool confession of faith was sufficiently clear to give
me confidence of sins forgiven and eternal life until I reached
early adolescence. Then I experienced what I call a "crisis of
confirmation." In a church without a formal confirmation ritual, I
worked through to an affirmation and confirmation of my commitment to Christ. The agony of doubt as I wondered, "Have I
really received Christ?" brought cold sweat to my forehead
through long and urgent altar calls. It was my perceptive mother
who understood my anguish, and she took me—not back to my
earlier experience, not to a reassuring assessment of "signs of
grace" in my life—she took me to the Word of God.

I remember turning with her to Romans 10:9 KJV, a verse so
familiar to me I could have quoted it:

> That if thou shalt confess with thy mouth the Lord Jesus, and shalt
> believe in thine heart that God hath raised him from the dead, thou
> shalt be saved.

"Tell me," Mother said, "who is Jesus Christ?"

"He's the Son of God . . . He's Lord!" I confessed, verbally.

"And do you believe that God raised Jesus from the dead?"

"Yes," I affirmed.

"Then, what does God say about your condition?"

"He says . . . I am saved!"

Even as I write these lines, twenty years later, the thrill of that assurance, of that ultimate confidence, runs through me.

Believing is a process that, for children in Christian homes, begins very early, and goes on to maturation. In the preschool years, a foundation can be laid for saving faith: by helping children gain correct—if not complete—concepts of God; by teaching them about the Lord Jesus Christ; by aiding their developing awareness of self and of sin—and then by giving them the opportunity to invite Jesus Christ into their lives as Saviour and Lord. Then comes the careful tending of that childhood faith by prayer and teaching, until, like the patient husbandman, we see "the precious fruit" of mature commitment (James 5:7 KJV).

Part II
CHARACTER

Character—an internalized structure of values which governs behavior—is an important emphasis in the Christian home. Without character, both confidence and creativity can be wasted on meaningless or even malicious activities.

The next few chapters deal with the development of character within the context of the Christian home.

8

Not Just Confidence—Character

To us as parents is entrusted the vital task of character development—of imprinting the distinctive stamp of godliness upon the lives of our children.

- A young woman discusses her future with us. "I'd like to go into full-time work, but I have a basic lack in me somewhere. I have lots of ideas, but I seem to lack the carry-through or determination to get them into action. My ideas sort of wither on the vine." We pray with her and for her, our hearts sad for a young person who has not had childhood training in the carrying out of tasks to completion.
- A young man is a promising preacher. He rightly divides the word of truth (2 Timothy 2:15) and his people are fed on the deep things of God. But when he leaves the town in which he has been minister, the name of Christ is disgraced and the church embarrassed by debts with local businesses that he has failed to clean up. All the confidence and training can't make up for a basic character lack. He is a dishonest man.
- A young missionary can't seem to get anything done. It's not that he's not bright or capable. It's just that, well—only his wife knows for sure, but others suspect. He can't get up in the morning and can't keep his mind on his work. Let's face it: he's dedicated and trained. But he's lazy.
- A young person is in charge of the Christian Education program in a church. The young people show up for announced executive meetings, but he doesn't. He's scheduled to speak and arrives unprepared. The morale of the young people falters as the kids see what the adults take longer to discover: he's irresponsible.

If you have been long in church circles, you know another list of sad stories you could add to these: young people whose hearts desire to serve God but whose characters are oddly out of sorts with their aims. Young people who somehow, somewhere, missed some basic character training. In the interest of shortening our lists of sad stories, I challenge Christian parents: It is not enough to raise your children with confidence. It is not enough to lead them to trusting faith in Jesus Christ. It is not enough to hope and pray that the Holy Spirit will transform sneaky, lazy little kids into mighty soldiers of the cross. To us as parents is entrusted the vital task of character development—of imprinting the distinctive stamp of godliness upon the lives of our children; of giving them moral direction to match the courage we have already discussed.

After all, one of the greatest sources of confidence to anybody is to know that he can distinguish between right and wrong and choose the right; to know that he can undertake a job and see it to satisfactory completion; to know that others can safely depend upon him. And while we may think that such qualities are exclusively the work of the Holy Spirit, we must understand that God works through human instruments, and in the lives of our children He works through us to bring to maturity people of God who have not only confidence but character, too.

The development of character begins in the very early years of life with our little one. Some psychologists believe that the basic character of the child has been shaped by the time he is five years of age. We will, in the preschool years, be shaping our children in three distinct ways: by example; by instruction; and by training.

Example will be the most important component in this trilogy of teaching methods. Children who see self-indulgent parents acting out their roles in adult life will learn to put themselves first. Children who see or hear parents discuss cheating on laws, from income tax to speed limits, will learn to treat the law of the land with contempt or light regard. Children will learn attitudes toward their daily work. Do parents accept work as a gift from God, to be done cheerfully and "as unto the Lord Christ"? Or do they drag themselves out, complaining and unthankful, to do the things demanded of them in the day? How do parents treat unpleasant chores? By indefinite postponement? By complainingly undertaking them? Or by quiet determination? Whatever attitude parents show will be reproduced in the child's character.

Teaching is the next method of shaping character. The Bible is the most important source of character delineation. Story after story shows the nature of man in his character—the disastrous results of flawed character and the good results of strong character. Children who grow up admiring Joseph, for instance, for his ability to say no to immorality; Daniel for his ability to say no to the king's meat and wine; Jesus for His ability to say no to all the enticements of the devil, are children who will want to have that kind of courage themselves. But telling children what is right and what is wrong, or even reading it from the Bible, will have far less effect than you might hope unless it is accompanied by exemplary character in the parents. Whenever instruction runs counter to the example parents are setting, conflict is set up in the child's mind, and may completely block his ability to accept the precept that is being taught. Christian parents must continuously bring their lives to the plumb line of Scripture, begging God the Holy Spirit to go on transforming them into the image of Jesus Christ. Only thus will the example they set be in essential harmony with the great examples of Scripture. Only so will their children see clearly and without conflict the sort of people of whom God approves.

Finally, we will imprint our children with good character through careful *training*. Training is something different from teaching. "Teaching makes a child know and understand what he is to do; training influences him and sees that he does it. Teaching deals with his mind; training with his will," says Andrew Murray. He also makes the telling point, "Habits must precede principles. Habits influence the person by giving a certain bent and direction, by making the performance of certain acts easy and natural, and thus preparing the way for obedience from principle."[21]

It is in the area of habit formation that parents most definitely will shape their children's character. If good habits of action and response are developed, the result will be good character—or at least the strongest possible predilection toward good character.

"Could the young but realize how soon they will become mere

walking bundles of habits, they would give more heed to their conduct while in the plastic state,'' said philosopher and psychologist William James.[22] Since habits and attitudes are most easily shaped correctly in the first place, rather than corrected later, we need to ask ourselves, ''What are the basic character traits we want to foster, and how can these traits be fostered in tiny preschoolers, where the task is easiest and most important?''

1. Integrity. One of the most important character traits is integrity: honesty in word and honesty in action. It is the mark of an ''integrated'' person—one who is not putting up false fronts, not pretending to be something he is not, not telling lies to cover up or distort; one whose word is his bond. The person of integrity is the kind of person who can let his yea be yea and his nay, nay (James 5:12), and who doesn't need to say anything more to bind himself. He is, as the Psalmist put it, the man who ''. . . swears to his own hurt, and does not change'' (Psalms 15:4 NAS). He is the kind of person who fills in credit-card applications accurately and income-tax forms truthfully. He is the kind of person who is *real*. This kind of person can be depended upon, for having accepted a job, he accomplishes it. If he says he'll be there at ten o'clock, that's when he'll arrive!

All of this sounds great, but how do we set the stage for this development?

(a) By telling our children the truth, always. We must avoid half answers to children's honest questions or untruthfulness in our own talk with others. How quickly the children catch on to our little ''social lies'' and discover that truth is not strictly necessary if it is embarrassing. This kind of parental honesty includes drawing a clear line between make-believe, imaginative pretending, and honesty. Parents should not lead their children to believe untruths, even as a form of teasing—or, as with Santa Claus, of play. Children are wonderful at entering the world of ''Let's pretend'' and are able to imagine endlessly. But they should know where imagining starts and reality stops. And they should have that line clearly drawn by parental example.

(b) By insistence on truthfulness in the child. Every child will attempt to lie, usually in self-defense to ''cover up''—particularly if he thinks he is about to get into trouble. Parents need to make a clear line between truth and lying in their children's communications. Punishment for a lie should be more severe than punishment for any other offense.

I used to question my children, looking straight into their eyes. "Are you telling me true words? It is most important that you tell me true words *always,* otherwise I can't trust what you tell me *ever."* Usually a child betrays his guilt or attempt to cover up. There is nothing wrong with saying, "I don't blame you for being afraid to tell me, because this is a mess and I'm pretty mad. But you must tell me the truth even when you are afraid." You may have to reassure a child. "If you tell me exactly what happened, I won't spank you this time. But if I find out that you have not told me true words, I will certainly have to spank."

(c) Insisting on truth in action. A child who helps himself to a neighbor child's toy must be taught that taking what is someone else's is stealing. A child must learn to "just look" in stores. If a child does take something that belongs to someone else—even if it is as little as an apple from your neighbor's apple tree—deal with the matter seriously. Apology must be offered by the child. Restoration or restitution must be made where possible. The parent who explains away a child's petty theft leaves the field of property ownership without the moral demarcation laid down in Scripture.

2. Responsibility. It is the parents' job to see that a task given to a child is carried through satisfactorily, whatever that task may be: putting his shoes under his bed; carrying out simple one-action commands such as picking up toys, or more complex tasks such as tidying up his room. Parents must not be too busy to see to it that the task is completed, and completed satisfactorily for the level of competence of which the child is capable. There doesn't have to be yelling and misery here, just firm insistence that the task assigned be carried out thoroughly and completely.

3. Submission to God-ordained authority. This will start at home. Only the child who has learned to submit to parental authority is likely to learn to submit to others. Judge Robert N. Conroy, a provincial court judge in the city of Saskatoon, told a prayer-breakfast fellowship:

On Monday morning I will go into my courtroom and see perhaps
sixty young people. I am willing to bet that not more than one or two
parents will be there. And when I open a new case, I will ask for a
presentence report on the past of the young offender. Before I ever
read the report, I can tell you what it will say: "So-and-So never
learned to submit to authority at home; couldn't take discipline at
school and dropped out early; resisted the authority of the boss on
the job; rebelled against the authority of the law."

It's all of one piece. From a strictly spiritual perspective, children
who learn to obey their parents find it much easier to learn to
obey God in their lives—and that is surely the long-range goal of
obedience training.

4. Self-control. Here a wide number of character traits come into
play: control of temper and angry responses; control of overeat-
ing or other indulgences; control of one's urges in many areas.
Training for self-control begins with the parent who firmly refuses
to get up for night feedings after the baby is old enough to sleep
the night, and proceeds through firm toilet training. It goes on in a
number of ways: not allowing children to throw temper tantrums
is basic, as is not letting them slam doors or in other angry,
violent ways express their displeasure. We have never let our
children scream in play. A scream is an emergency call and has
to be saved for that. Because our children have not screamed at
high pitch or cried overnoisily, we know when to rush to their aid
if there is a true emergency. We have rejected play becoming
unpleasantly noisy in the house or car. But of course our children
have shouted themselves hoarse out of doors.

Children should not be allowed to hit, pinch, bite, or otherwise
hurt each other. A child who repeatedly pinches, scratches, or
bites other children should have the experience of a firm and
judiciously applied pinch or scratch or bite. Just once, with the
explanation, "This is how it feels," cures most little meanies.
This is basic civilizing; it requires and results in self-control.
Then, too, there is no need for a child to cry noisily, after a hurt
or punishment, or for an unduly extended period of time. "That
will do, now," can be a firm and reasonable demand for self-
control. Learning to "boss your body" has long-term and multi-
ple implications—and self-control is essential to anyone who de-

sires, like Paul, to keep the body from controlling the spirit (1 Corinthians 9:27).

5. *Self-discipline*. Ultimately, this is the answer to laziness, lack of ambition, lack of follow-through. It is the long-term outcome of consistent discipline in the home. Self-discipline is the coil spring which can power all kinds of productivity. It is learned through positive discipline: the required tasks done to completion, the years of schoolwork done well, the music lessons. Eight years of piano lessons didn't teach me a lot about music but did teach me a lot about *sitting*—and that discipline I have been able to transfer to writing. A young woman commented to me, "I don't have the self-discipline to bring my creativity to fruition. I wish my parents had made me do some things!"

6. *Reverence to God and respect for others*. A revival was sweeping through a large church. Young people were confessing their sins in public testimony meetings. People were excited. But one of the elders said quietly, "There has not yet been any deep work of God in the hearts of these young people."

"What do you mean?" another elder asked, surprised. "We're hearing wonderful reports."

"Yes," said the senior elder. "But I saw the church gym after those young people used it the other night. Candy wrappers and paper littered throughout, with no attempt to pick them up. When the Spirit of God touches those young people, this kind of thing won't happen."

If we love God, if we are truly in tune with Him, we will never take lightly our responsibilities to others. If we revere God, we will respect other people and their property. If we have an awe of God, it will govern the way we find wiener sticks at the picnic park, the care with which we extinguish a camp fire, and the tone of voice with which we greet our neighbors. God declared about all of His creation, from man to the universe, that it was, in His eyes, "very good" (Genesis 1:31 KJV). Creation bears God's stamp. The person who learns to say, "Our Father," as Jesus taught (Luke 11:2 KJV) is never a person who dares to be careless about either the people or physical resources of his environment.

The Book of Proverbs is a handbook on character. Parents who want to develop character in their children should apply themselves to that book—and then apply the principles to their children. For without character, all of the confidence and all of the creativity will be as water poured out upon the ground. Wasted lives are the result of carelessness in the training of character.

9

Discipline for Self-Discipline

It is in the home that the child learns the basic principle of accountability for actions: first to those around him, and ultimately to God.

The young mother repeatedly interrupted our telephone conversation. "You run along now, Donnie," she said to her four-
year-old whose demanding voice formed a background to our
chat. A couple of minutes later, "Donnie, I told you to go and
play." And later again, "Now you go to your room and
play . . . ." The child was noisily defying her, just beyond her
reach.

"For goodness sake, Kay," I said, "don't just stand there. *Do*
something."

"What should I do? He just defies me."

"Kay," I said, "you should hang up the phone, walk over to
that child, and pick him up and paddle him."

"With my hand?"

"Sure."

"Do you really think I should?"

"Yes. I really think you should—now."

The phone clicked dead. It rang again a few minutes later. "I
did it," Kay said, sounding a little awed at herself. "And it
worked. He's playing like a lamb."

"Sure," I said. "Just do that after the first time he's defiant,
instead of waiting for the fifteenth. It will be easier on everyone."

But Kay was still questioning. "At that family-life seminar we
went to, the speaker said you should never strike a child with
your hand."

"Oh?" I said.

"He said the hand of the parent should be a hand of love."

"Love includes chastening," I reminded her.

77

"Yeah. Well he said we should always use something else—a belt or a wooden spoon—so the child wouldn't come to fear our hand."

"And how many kids did the speaker have?" I asked.

"None."

"Look, Kay. I don't think a child makes that distinction. It's going to be your hand whether it's holding a belt or not. With really little children, what's important is that chastisement is swift and sure. And if you lose precious minutes trying to find your 'spanking machine,' you are losing opportunities."

We talked at length about the whole business of discipline. In the months that followed, as Kay and her husband began to put into effect a program of consistent and firm discipline, I saw their young family of preschoolers transformed from an unruly little mob to three ebullient but manageable youngsters.

Kay's indecision, confusion, and hence ineffectiveness is all too typical of parents today. All tied up with dos and don'ts, many parents fail to recognize and put into effect basic principles of good discipline.

First of all, we need to widen our understanding of discipline. It is a broad term, and in a good home it will mean far more than merely punishing. *Discipline is training which corrects, molds, strengthens, or perfects.*[23] When we talk about discipline, we are talking about a whole range of important, life-shaping events. The end results of a well-executed program of discipline in the home are harmony for the family unit and self-discipline for the individual child. These results are too far-reachingly significant for us to gamble on ever-changing psychological theories. For the principles behind a good program of discipline, we must turn to the Word of God. Only then can we proceed confidently in this important area.

In the Word of God, as we have seen earlier, parental authority is clearly laid out. Parents must exercise their authority under God, and children must obey their parents. As I have explained to my little ones, "We all have to obey God. God tells you to obey your parents. That's your job. And He tells us to make sure that you do obey us. That's our job." Thus I endeavored to communicate to them the scriptural pattern: parents and children alike, we are accountable to God for our actions.

Our children need us to exercise our authority in discipline if they are to develop into mature and confident people. And they need it in order to be happy during childhood. The disciplined child is a reassured and confident child. He knows the limitations of his environment and is secure within them. Even if he is one of those children who always pushes at the boundaries, he is secure because he knows there are boundaries and they are firm. At its best, discipline says to the child, "I love you too much to let you be a little monster." And the child who is disciplined reflects the happiness of a reassured, loved child (Hebrews 12:6–11).

Second, the child who is disciplined is a child who does not carry an unnecessary load of guilt around. We must remember that when we deal with children we are not dealing with little blobs which come to us without will and without direction. As fallen creatures, they are born with a tendency to do wrong, and a will that is bent against authority. In the book *Passages,* Gail Sheehy writes:

> Each child arrives in the world an outlaw. He strives to center the universe about himself and to make it what he wants it to be: his own inner circle.[24]

This observation by a secular writer is certainly in line with the testimony of Scripture, "Behold, I was shapen in iniquity" (Psalms 51:5 KJV), or "Foolishness is bound up in the heart of a child; The rod of discipline will remove it far from him" (Proverbs 22:15 NAS). Ultimately, the cure for this tendency to selfishness and sin will be in the child's personal regeneration through faith in the Lord Jesus Christ. But as parents, we can make preparation for that inner change by correcting the framework of behavior.

A child who has not answered for the wrongs he has done does not understand elementary justice. The home is where the human learns that wrongs committed must be punished. It is in the home that the child learns the basic principle of accountability for actions: first to those around him (in the early years, his parents), and ultimately, to God. It is only within the godly home where discipline is exercised in "the fear of the Lord," that the child learns that sin is *against* God and *before* man—a perception uttered by the returning Prodigal who cried out to his welcoming father, ''Father, I have sinned against heaven, and in thy sight . . . '' (Luke 15:21 KJV).

It is through discipline that the child comes to understand the meaning of and relief from ''true moral guilt.'' Because as Christians we believe that there is such a thing as ''true moral guilt'' as opposed to ''guilt feelings,'' we know that it is important for our children to acknowledge and accept the consequences of their wrongdoings.[25] In our children's lives, as in the life of mankind as a whole, ''The law [is] our schoolmaster to bring us unto Christ, that we might be justified by faith (Galatians 3:24 KJV).

I have seen a child of mine utterly miserable until he has confessed and taken a fair punishment for something wrong which he has done—and then suddenly released and happy. Why? He knew that wrong has a consequence, and he is freed from the guilt of that wrong when he takes the consequence for it. Unpunished children are guilt-miserable.

Children who understand that if they trespass the parental word they will be punished are reassured and at peace with themselves. They, therefore, can also be at peace with each other. And so the result of a good program of discipline is a peaceful family. Now I am not suggesting that there will not be times when parent and child clash. But the overall tone of a home should be happy, relaxed, at peace. There should be purposeful, meaningful activity joined in with a minimum of clash between differing personalities. And this will only happen when the children are disciplined.

A good program of discipline will gradually make itself obsolete. Indeed, the child who has been well disciplined by spanking may, by the time he is five or six, never need a physical encounter with his parents again. Certainly by the time he is eight or nine, he should have had his last spanking. I am not talking about trying to spank adolescent children: that is usually a too-late expedient and results in smoldering anger and rebellion. A good program of discipline results in the establishment of a relationship between parent and child in line with that which the Scriptures endorse: the parental word respectfully obeyed, even if it is not entirely agreed with. Discussion follows obedience rather than preceding it, and there is harmony in the home.

I have spoken of a "good program" of discipline. I will outline one now, not because I think I have all the answers but because I encounter so many parents who have none, and read so much literature which can only confuse and disturb parents who are attempting to use biblical guidelines in their own homes.

1. A good program of discipline starts with the self-discipline of the parent. Just as instilling confidence begins with parental confidence, so exercising discipline in the home begins with parental self-discipline. Parents who cannot discipline themselves to discipline their children will always fail in this area. "I know the children are naughty," one young mother complained. "But I'm so tired all the time. I just don't have the energy to deal with them." The young mother who has recently given birth to her third or fourth baby and who has a clutch of little ones around her has my complete empathy. I've been there. But I know that the smallest expediture of energy is that spent in discipline: it alleviates the need for huge additional expenditures—cleaning up foolish and unnecessary messes or breakages; yelling and scolding and pleading. The mother who is firm and fair, who disciplines quickly and thoroughly, is the mother who is saving herself the most energy. Burton L. White summarizes observation of many children in many home situations in *The First Three Years of Life.* He says:

> In the homes . . . where children are developing well . . . we have always seen mothers run the home with a loving but firm hand. The babies in these home situations rarely have any question about who is the final authority . . . . We have very rarely seen the most effective mothers repeat anything more than once in the way of a restriction or a control sentence. If a child did not respond in the desired way after the message was repeated once, the mother acted . . . .[26]

Obviously, such discipline requires continuous self-discipline on the part of the parent.

2. A good program of discipline begins early. The letter from my friend said, "Timmy is two, and the doctor says he can understand a spanking now." I think my friend was getting a late start—although better late than never. Whether or not a child can understand the whole significance of a spanking until he is— perhaps—an adult, is irrelevant. The fact is that spanking is an effective method of simple negative reinforcement of nondesirable behavior by as early as six months. Between six and nine months, a child can learn the simple avoidance reaction: "If I touch that big plant, I experience discomfort. So, being a bright little kid, I will not touch that big plant." Children's lives should not be cluttered with "no nos." But neither should everything a child may not touch be moved from a room. That approach creates a situation in which the child becomes the dominant member of the household. I am all for inquiring, exploring children; I am also for children who learn that not everything is theirs to play with, to handle, to hurt. From the time the child begins to crawl around, he begins to express his own interests—and these are often at variance with his parents' wishes. It is at that point that the first meaningful discipline of a negative sort can be put into effect.

Prior to this, other disciplines are workable: allowing a child to cry for a few minutes before going to sleep; allowing a child to cry for a couple of nights in order to cut out a night feeding; being firm about putting the child down for nap times and bedtimes. These are also places where the parental will and the child's will may be at odds, and it is important that the child be cared for, loved, and reassured, but treated firmly and made a part of the family—not only a "voice crying in the wilderness," demanding continuous and constant attention. A child who is still interrupting his mother's sleep every night beyond three or four months is probably a child who has not met firm enough discipline—unless he has a specific health problem which needs attention.

How do you discipline a child of under a year—a child who is not yet talking? Very simply. The child begins to wriggle, swim, crawl—whatever his method of locomotion is—toward something you have decided he should not touch: your big rubber plant, perhaps, or the modular wall unit where your stereo components are kept. You pay attention to the child (that is where self-discipline comes in). As he reaches for the item, you simply say, "No." The child does not respond to your words: perhaps at this early stage he does not understand them, and reaches anyhow. You slap the back of his hands—not hard, but sharply enough that he can feel it—and repeat, "No." It will take very few repeats of this association of physical discomfort with the word *no* for him to respond to the word itself. And half the game of disciplining is won—before the child is one!

There is nothing wrong with supplying alternatives to a child; nothing wrong with removing him from the tempting items—as long as it is accompanied with the teaching of obedience to the parental voice. Learning to respect a parent's "No" is a big step toward overall obedient behavior. It makes a child manageable in any new circumstance: shopping in a store; visiting in another person's home; waiting in a doctor's office. In any of these settings, an obedient child is much more manageable than a child who has lived without limits.

"No" does not imply a judgment about wrongness or evil of the child's behavior; it simply says, "I say no. You may not do that because I have decided you cannot." The purpose is to establish the parental word of command. For that reason I prefer it over such words as *naughty* or *bad* which should be saved as labels for actually naughty behavior, when a child deliberately chooses to do wrong. While an early start makes life better for both parents and child, "better late than never" in applying firm and consistent discipline to the child is still a good rule.

3. A good program of discipline includes both negative and positive elements. As the child's responses and behaviors become increasingly complex, the program of discipline must develop, too. Always the establishment of the authority of the parental word is the short-range goal; the development of internal self-discipline is the long-range goal. To this end both negative and positive discipline is necessary. *Positive discipline includes:*

(a) Training in competencies from toilet use to self-feeding to putting on clothes.

(b) Training in household chores from picking up toys to keeping one's own room tidy and presentable.

(c) Training in daily courtesies such as "please" and "thank you"; a measure of quiet when adults are visiting; sharing toys with others; being courteous to siblings.

(d) Training in self-control. Crying is permissible, but not loud, uncontrolled sobbing; disappointment can be shown without long thundercloud periods; uncontrollable laughing or tantrums may be equally undesirable; voices can be kept quiet, and impatience near mealtime can be spoken of rather than demonstrated.

(e) Completion of tasks given. Tasks given should be suited to the child—if they prove to be simply above the child's ability, the parent should assist the child to bring the task to successful completion.

We have already talked about methods of training which include command, demonstration, and insistence of follow-through. By careful training, many kinds of disciplinary action of the negative kind can simply be eliminated. However, since our children are sons of Adam before they become sons of God, we must face the necessity of *negative* or *corrective discipline* as well:

(a) Correcting the child by word. This is the first level of negative discipline—and as the child matures it should replace the more severe measures listed below in the list. Our aim in discipline is to make the child increasingly responsive to our word. The use of physical force is only to reinforce the authority of our word. When a child disobeys, or refuses, or simply neglects to carry out a command, the first level of correction is verbal: "Johnny, I told you to pick up your toys." The parental word should be judicious, nonabusive, and directed at the behavior rather than at the child—so that it builds rather than destroys that important element of confidence. The fewer the words, the better. Let our words be carefully chosen and said firmly, and if at all possible, quietly. I doubt if there are any parents who do not sometimes raise their voices at their children. But it should be the exception, not the rule—the way in which the voice is used in extreme exasperation, not the way it is used in normal, judicious discipline patterns.

Threatening the child is unwise, but there is a difference between threatening, "If you scratch baby, I'll beat the tar out of you," and forewarning a child of consequences. "You must not scratch the baby. That hurts her. If I ever find you hurting the baby again, I will have to spank you." There are ample scriptural precedents for giving advance notice of consequences (Deuteronomy 28). The key here is your own disciplined follow-through. Consequences promised must be fulfilled.

(b) Spanking. When the parental word has been disobeyed, when a verbal admonition is not heeded—then spanking should be administered immediately. Let me be specific about spanking. I am not talking about slapping, about beating, about kicking; I am not talking about any method that could be remotely related to child abuse. "Slapping around" is dangerous and dehumanizing. So is kicking, shaking, or pulling a child around roughly. Parents will answer to God for any violent abuse of their children. Spanking, however, is a judicious action, the firm application of the hand (or wide, flat belt or wooden spoon), to the child's bottom. Spanking of this kind is traumatic, to be sure. Traumatic enough for the parent that he does not apply it more often than necessary. Traumatic enough for the child that he quickly learns behavior patterns which enable him to avoid spankings.

Up to the age of three or so, the spanking should be administered promptly and on the scene, so that the child can make the exact connection between the undesirable action and the unpleasant parental reaction. The spanking must, to be effective, be felt. Little is gained by a tap buffered by three thicknesses of diapers.

After a child is three, spankings should not be administered publicly. The child should not be humiliated in front of friends or siblings. He should be taken to his room where the nature of his misbehavior can be briefly but clearly stated. I think it is a good idea to decide how many strokes you are going to apply, proportionate to the seriousness of the offense, before you begin the spanking. That way you will not carry on in satisfaction of your own anger.

Most often, the child should be spanked for behavior which is disobedient to the parental command; deliberately and knowledgeably naughty; dangerous to either the child or another.

All of us who have families know that some children correct easily and quickly; some are more determined to have their own way and are correspondingly more difficult to correct. But all children need some correction. And that is the parents' duty. I didn't give my children long lectures before spankings, but I did identify the naughty behavior and explain, "I am going to spank you to help you remember not to do that again." Our children understood that spanking was both punishment for an offense and training in behavior. They knew that the quicker they learned the desirable behavior, the quicker they could avoid the spanking. Spankings may be a common part of the daily scene where there are several preschoolers in the house. But spankings must be reasonable, intelligible to the child, and fair, in order to preclude the building up of resentments.

I don't recommend that the child be hugged and comforted immediately after the spanking. He should be left until he comes back to the parent with words or actions that say, "I'm sorry. Receive me again." Then the parent should respond as did the father of the Prodigal Son—moving out toward the child in love and full acceptance.

When the child gets to be about six, he will probably want to enter a defense before a spanking. I think he should be listened to, with the parent making a careful judgment. Parents, too, are human, and capable of error. We have, at times, had to apologize to our children for having been hasty or too harsh.

Some confrontations can be avoided by allowing for discussion before the parental word of command is spoken. But once the word has been spoken, compliance must follow.

(c) Withdrawal of privilege. As the child grows older, it is important for him to learn that wrongdoing not only incurs punishment but also has its own consequences. Withdrawal of a privilege, related as nearly as possible to the misdemeanor, is often a wise alternative to spanking.

What sort of privileges can be withdrawn from a preschooler? Going to the store for shopping; having dessert (going to bed without dessert is quite impressive); watching a favorite TV show; having a story read by a parent.

Because the withdrawal of privilege is a more complex form of discipline than spanking, I do not see it as the primary method for preschool children. As children get older, it plays an increasing role in teaching responsibility. But in the preschool years, the duration of the punishment may cause resentment. The lack of one-to-one relationship with the misdemeanor may cause confusion as well.

I have been appalled to read some handbooks on child rearing which suggest that effective use in discipline can be made of the withdrawal of parental love. The same books which suggest that spanking is barbaric and cruel offer this suggestion of much more subtle and damaging cruelty. To me, punishing or threatening a child with the withdrawal of love is insupportable. As an adult, I am secure in the steadfast love of God my Father because as a child, I was secure in the unending love of my parents. "Jesus loves me when I'm bad, though it makes Him very sad," expresses a very important principle.

We do not love the child less when we are spanking him than when we are hugging him. It is just that his behavior elicits that particular manifestation of our love which he receives. We must discipline firmly, frequently, and, to the best of our judgment, fairly. But we must not hold our anger toward our children. They must go to sleep assured of our love.

4. Discipline leads to self-discipline on the part of the child. Ultimately, the goal of discipline is to make the child a self-disciplining, responsible entity. The outcome is children who are "inner directed" by means of what sociologist David Riesman calls metaphorically "a psychological gyroscope."

> This instrument, once it is set by the parents . . . keeps the inner-directed person . . . "on course" even when tradition . . . no longer dictates his moves. The inner-directed person becomes capable of maintaining a delicate balance between the demands upon him of his life goal and the buffetings of his external environment . . . . Since the direction to be taken in life has been learned in the privacy of the home from a smaller number of guides, and since principles, rather than details of behavior, are internalized, the inner-directed person is capable of great stability.[27]

Setting within our children a "psychological gyroscope" set to the course indicated by the Word of God must be considered one of the most important tasks of Christian parenting.

As children edge out of the preschool years, the responsibility for choosing behaviors should be gradually laid on them. Not, "Wear your coat, Timmy," but "It's cool this morning. What do you think you should wear outside?" Only if the child shows himself incapable of making appropriate choices should parental authority direct. Gradually, the child should be invited to exercise self-discipline, to act out the inner-directedness.

Scriptural principles understood and applied lead us to some different conclusions from those which are suggested by non-Christian psychologists and writers today. Recognizing that our authority and responsibility is from God; understanding the implications of the fallen nature of man; guiding our children toward obedience to God through obedience to us; reassuring our children of our steadfast love: these things will be important as we discipline our children toward the desired end of full self-discipline.

10

A Firm Foundation

The centrality of Scripture in the Christian family is a cherished tradition for many of us; but it will only continue if we are faithful in passing it on to our children.

"What should be the distinctives of Christian family life?" Sheila raised the question, one she had been discussing with the other members of her Bible-study group.

I jotted notes on a page in my coil notebook as we tossed ideas back and forth. As I read our list now, picking it out from the doodles and extra notes, I see that we suggested the following areas in which the Christian family should be distinguishable from others:

commitment and fidelity in marriage
servant leadership within home
discipline
hospitality and sharing
restraint and moderation in life-style
priority given to church involvement
sharing of faith, values, and truth through Scripture reading and
    prayer

The last two items on that list constitute the laying of a firm foundation for the spiritual and moral development of our children.

Those of us with small children are members of a "hang loose" generation, with a primary emphasis on "doing your own thing." And there is the danger that we may lose sight of the importance in our own lives and in those of our children of having close bonds with other believers within a church fellowship. As a "community of faith,'' the church should represent an extension of family life and caring to our children. According to Zuck and Clark:

> The congregation . . . ought to be an extended family, a tribe, or a network of intimate circles of mutual concern, sharing, and faith . . . . The very dynamics of relationships in the nuclear family make it imperative that the "tribe" furnish some of the models and reinforce the parental values if they are to prevail. The congregation, through its informal and formal ministries, is uniquely prepared to contribute significantly to the child's Christian decision making and growth because it is transgenerational in character, relational in essence, and has abundant resources for both didactic and modeling instruction.[28]

Not long ago, the pastor in our local church asked the children, "Why do you come to church?"

Little Wade's hand shot up. "Because it's Sunday and because we like to come," was his answer. And a good one. It expressed church attendance as both a *routine discipline* and a *special joy* in his family's life. And church attendance needs to be both if it is to contribute to our family life. "I'm so glad I'm a part of the family of God," should be a song our children can sing, with a deep, personal understanding of a church fellowship which represents that larger family to him.

But while the church has a very important part to play in Christian family life, the full burden of the transmission of Christian truth and values can never be laid upon it. At best, church activities will only occupy two or three hours each week. So the teaching of the church will be most effective only when it reinforces and reiterates teaching which is going on in the home on a day-to-day basis.

Paul tells Timothy that food is "sanctified by the word of God and prayer" (1 Timothy 4:5 KJV). And so it should be in our homes. Grace before meals is, of course, basic. But mealtimes also provide a natural gathering together of the family when the Scriptures can be read. With our family, breakfast has been the best time for reading and prayer together. The evening meal may be more suitable to others. What is important is that the Bible be read together daily. Scripture reading and prayer together should be a joyful routine in Christian family life.

All the helpful hints on how to have happy family devotions have, I think, made parents feel they have to plan a program in order to share the Scriptures with their children. The sad result is that most just get tired thinking about it—or have a few flops— and quit. It just does not need to be that complicated. "The word of God and prayer": a short passage, a short prayer. That, made a part of at least one meal a day, is far better than an elaborate family worship held once in a while.

Writing of Jonathan Edwards's home life, Elisabeth D. Dodds says:

> One source of the family stability was the steady dependable routine of prayers which they had together, before breakfast and again after supper. Edwards' choice of Scripture [showed him to be] partial to the poetic books of the Bible . . . . The surge and thunder of the King James Bible, heard twice a day aloud in their father's voice, became part of the children's earliest memories.[29]

The centrality of Scripture in the Christian family is a cherished tradition for many of us; but it will only continue if we are faithful in passing it on to our children. "Isn't it hard on little children to have to sit through a Bible reading once or twice a day?" many parents ask. "Won't they come to resent it?" Obviously, Bible reading should not be prolonged with little children. My father used to read ten verses ("even if that left him midparagraph," my mother remembers). So Scripture reading was not tediously long. With modern speech translations set out in paragraphs instead of verses, it is easy to read a "thought unit"—a paragraph or two—with children.

I remember being startled when a young minister who had visited in my parents' home asked me, "How did you kids feel about having to read the Bible every day?" How did we feel about it? Well, for one thing, we were never asked. It was a part of family life that was as unquestionable as breakfast itself. And my parents made us aware that the Bible was special, a gift that had come to us at great cost. On long winter evenings when we were very young, my mother read us stories such as *Great Was the Company* and *Mary Jones and Her Bible*. Missionary stories gave us a look at cultures untouched by the Gospel. A little history, a little geography: it all helped us value the Scriptures we heard. Our parents' attitude of reverence for the Word and gratitude for its availability became ours.

I can identify strongly with the passionate love for Scripture expressed by David Lurie, the growing-up-Jewish hero of Chaim Potok's *In the Beginning*. As David joins in the synagogue celebration at completion of the year's cycle of readings from the Torah, he wonders about his Gentile, nominally Christian, friends:

> The joy of dancing with the Torah, holding it close to you, the words of God to Moses at Sinai. I wondered if gentiles ever danced with their Bible. "Hey, Tony. Do you ever dance with your Bible? . . . Do you ever read your Bible? Do you ever hold it to you and know how much you love it?" [30]

If our children are to learn to love the Lord, they must learn to love the Word that reveals Him to us. And, let's face it: they will not only be spiritually impoverished but also culturally and intellectually impoverished if we fail to transmit the Bible with all its wealth of precept and principle and story and example to them.

The question of what passages to read with preschoolers is important. Some parents flounder at this point, and finally give up, hopelessly bogged down in genealogies in Numbers! With our preschoolers, we majored on the poetry of Psalms and Proverbs, the wonderful Old Testament stories, and the Gospels. I made a scrapbook of "Proverbs for Little People," with selected proverbs printed beside bright magazine pictures illustrating the message. In another scrapbook, I pasted illustrations for selected Psalms (23, 24, 131, and 148). These books the children quite literally wore out with reading and handling.

The Old Testament stories we read as serializations, a short episode at a time. The stories of David (1 and 2 Samuel) and of Daniel and his friends emerged as favorites, requested over and over again. The "family stories" of Genesis, the stories of the Judges, and of the Prophets Elijah and Elisha (1 and 2 Kings) are also good listening for little children. Of the Gospels, Mark is perhaps the most suitable for very young children, with its fast-paced narrative. But Luke places a much-loved emphasis on the birth and boyhood of our Lord. The other Gospels, too, are interesting—but they have more doctrinal and interpretive content.

Since "All Scripture is God-breathed and is useful for teaching, rebuking, correcting and training in righteousness" (2 Timothy 3:16 NEW INTERNATIONAL VERSION), as children grow older they should be given the opportunity to read together the whole Bible. A complete understanding is probably less important than a careful implanting of the Word. For if the Word really takes root in our children's minds, the Holy Spirit can instruct them in its meanings and implications through all the years of their lives.

Beyond the daily routine of Scripture reading, Christian parents will find many opportunities to widen their children's experience with the Bible and its truths. Reading from storybooks and listening to records or tapes with the children are some possibilities. One of our preschoolers has listened, engrossed, to whole books of the Bible on the *Living Bible* cassettes. Role playing and informal dramatizations of many of the stories has been fun. For a few favorite stories I gave the children flannelgraph figures to work with.

The reciprocal of God's speaking to us in His Word is our speaking to God in prayer. And prayer should be an important aspect of Christian family living. Over and above the ritualized patterns of grace before meals and prayer after Bible reading, there are many times for spontaneous prayer.

I recall a day with Cammie-Lou, not yet four, in the "Windless Woods," a favorite little woods on our farm, where the tall trees held out the wind and created a place of complete stillness. The late summer was moving toward fall, and a few colored leaves had already drifted to the ground. Ants scurried at our feet as we sat together on a rot-softened log, peeling the moss back with our fingers. "Let's say thank you to God," Cammie suggested.

"Let's. But let's not shut our eyes. It's too beautiful for that." We prayed together, thanking God for each lovely thing we saw. And "eyes open" prayers became a part of our family's prayer repertoire.

Several years later, the girls ran in on a fall afternoon with a beautiful little bouquet of field flowers and grasses. They arranged them in a vase. Then Heather Ruth offered a Bambi candle to complete the centerpiece. We sat down at the table, just to look.

As Heather lit her candle, the aesthetic delight focused itself on
God, the giver of all good gifts. We began to praise the Lord
together in song—with both tune and words extemporaneous. I
sang a phrase, then one of the children offered a phrase, and
round our little fellowship circle we went, praising God for the joy
of our family, the beauty of His world, and the love of His Son.
We celebrated together the joy of life. And, in the words of C. S.
Lewis, our minds "ran back up the sunbeam to the sun." [31]

Our after-bedtime visits with the children usually include informal prayer. Cam most often makes the rounds, sitting on the
edge of each bed, visiting with each child individually, and closing
with a time of prayer. It is a way of incorporating closeness and
love with prayer in an intimate way.

It seemed natural to me to help the children pray about a problem on the spot, to ask forgiveness when they had done wrong, to
continuously offer up their praise and thanksgiving. But I found I
had to work more consciously at teaching them to pray about the
needs of others. Our family's friendship with missionary families
has been the main prompting to prayer for missions. We share
with our children current prayer letters as they arrive and have
special prayer for the needs of that particular missionary or family.

One young mother told me about the prayer program in her
home. Their coffee table had a glass top, under which were placed
pictures of missionary friends. When prayer time came, each
child was invited to choose a missionary to pray for. The child
would place his hand over the picture as he prayed for the people.
I think this is a beautiful way to teach children to intercede, to
identify with the needs of others.

A scrapbook of missionary pictures, maps showing their loca-
tion, and space for clippings from their letters is another good
prayer prompter. A family which supports a foster child in
another country can learn to pray for the personal needs of those
in our world who are materially deprived. Interceding on behalf of
friends and neighbors is something which children can enter into
earnestly and simply. Encouraging such prayer helps to develop
the attitude of concern and compassion which should mark Christian people.

Talking with God about daily joys, expressing our praise and gratitude, learning to pray in confession of sin, interceding for others; in all of these ways we can help our children to grow spiritually. And as we teach them, we will find ourselves making, again and again, the disciples' request, "Lord, teach us to pray" (Luke 11:1 KJV).

Making time for church attendance, Bible reading, and prayer is a task of primary importance for Christian parents. Not only our food but also the whole of family life should day-by-day be "sanctified by the word of God and prayer" (1 Timothy 4:5).

11

Handling the Great Competitor

Is our home controlling television, or is television controlling our home?

Sprawled on his stomach, chin in hand, he watches, enthralled. His day isn't complete without "Sesame Street." He counts television characters among his real friends. And he knows more about space exploration than his parents. Today's child has a source of instant entertainment and instant education at his fingertips. Few parents would question that TV has brought a world of learning into the living room which, carefully used, can greatly enrich the lives of their youngsters. Time and time again my children surprise me with their knowledge about some exotic place or process. "I saw it on TV," they explain with a shrug. Through television a child can explore the undersea world with Jacques Cousteau, attend the Olympics, and see his government officials.

Certainly I am not a mother to pit myself against TV on basic principle. Without children's morning educational programs ("Mr. Dressup" and "Sesame Street"), I would not have been able to write *Love, Honor and Be Free* or *Living on Less and Liking It More!* My manuscript work has customarily gotten underway each day about the same time as the hour of TV I have allotted to my preschoolers. But I do think it is very important to pose this question: Is our home controlling television, or is television controlling our home?

Here are some ways in which you can determine the answer to that question:

(1) Do you organize mealtimes around the television schedule? Are some or most mealtimes dominated by the television set?

(2) How many hours of television per day do your children

watch? (The average preschool viewing time is said to be fifty or more hours per week. It is now estimated that the average pre-schooler spends more time watching TV than in any other activity. Is this true of your preschoolers?) In any home where the television comes on with the signal patterns and stays on throughout the day, even if the children are not always solely watching television, they are being influenced by it for most of their waking hours.

(3) How much evening time do you and your spouse spend watching TV? In comparison with time spent visiting and entertaining? In reading? In real conversation? Many adults watch six hours of television per day; the all-round average is four hours per day. Would this be true of your family members?

(4) Do you have a planned systematic time for family Bible reading and prayer each day—at least once a day?

If you are not sure about the answers to these questions, keep a calendar for a month, noting hours of TV per family member, occasions for family worship, entertaining, and conversation. Then you can really answer the questions. Most people are shocked to discover exactly how much time television takes out of family living.

Before we bought our first TV set many years ago, we wanted to be sure that we could control it, and not have it control us. We determined that we would not turn on the TV unless both Cam and I had our devotional time. It worked wonderfully: we both got very faithful in having our devotions early in the day.

Let's look at several areas in which television acts as the "Great Competitor" within Christian homes—and some of the ways we can best handle it.

1. Values. Not long ago, I was discussing TV with an older Christian woman. I told her that I didn't watch afternoon movies because I did not want to expose my preschoolers to adultery, divorce, and violence.

"Oh, don't be so silly," she said. "You can't protect them from the world. They're going to go to school and learn all that." Her attitude was typical of many who excuse their own daytime viewing by begging the question of the effect on children of what they see. I protested that I could, and must, protect them from some aspects of the world's value system—at least in their most imprintable, value-formative years. She fired another shot: "Anyway, kids don't really watch TV. They get bored and play." But children learn not just when they are paying close attention, but constantly. Their basic mode of learning is "assimilation"— constantly taking in "bits and pieces" from which they form concepts.[32]

As Christian parents, we owe to our children homes which are a haven from the values of a corrupt and immoral society. To the extent that we turn child care over to the television set, we abdicate our responsibility. If our little tots watch the afternoon soap operas, and our older kids sit up and watch the evening programing, and our teenagers stay up for the late movies weekend after weekend, we should not be surprised to discover them with little heart for God, little concern for the needy, and a great deal of taste for the things of the world. We cannot hope to blot out the effects of hours and hours of TV watching even by regular family worship or a few earnest hours of church time on Sunday. The children will have absorbed the twisted values of this age, especially concerning sex and marriage and the importance of material things.

I was a deprived child. My parents didn't even let us go to an occasional movie—and they never did own a television set. We have deprived our children, too: of jokes that make fornication, adultery, and homosexuality appear to be funny instead of sinful; of plots that show marriages either falling apart or facilely happy; of endless commercials that pose material answers to all of life's deepest needs.

It might be worthwhile to analyze the content of TV programing viewed by your family for a week by the criteria of 1 John 2:15; 16 KJV: "Love not the world, neither the things that are in the world . . . . For all that is in the world,

the lust of the flesh   ("craze for sex"),
and the lust of the eyes   ("ambition to buy everything that appeals to you"),
and the pride of life   ("pride that comes from wealth and importance"),

is not of the Father, but is of the world." [33]

What is left over when you rule out those programs which depend for plot or humor or financial backing on appeals to sex, materialism, or ego gratification? The documentaries, perhaps, and public-affairs broadcasts. The nature programs. And the sports.

But even sports programing brings us to the second concern we should have as we consider the effect of TV watching on children's minds.

2. Violence. "Between the ages of five and thirteen, children see approximately 13,400 murders. They learn that violence is the way to express manliness and success." [34] What does such massive television exposure to violence do to our children? We do not yet fully know, but research evidence is mounting, and frightening.

First, there is the possibility of inducing imitative violence. Children are born imitators. They are bound to imitate their heroes. Not long ago, our children walked across a skyway in the city of Edmonton while we were visiting with friends. Two girls approached our children and in loud, abusive language, threatened to kill them. One had a hand in a pocket. "Don't move," she yelled. "I've got a gun here and I'll shoot." Our children outbluffed the girls, but came home rather shaken. Of course, the other children were just pretending—that time.

Increasing evidence shows that continuous exposure to violence may ultimately affect sanity. "Every murder or violent act a child witnesses on TV is like a small, even a mini-scale weight placed on the balance," Dr. Robert Lieber said in witness to a Canadian Royal Commission on Violence in the Communications Industry. "No psychologist would be able to guarantee that eventually the balance might not tip, triggering violent acts on the part of individuals who previously had appeared normal." [35]

Other studies show that the frequency with which children are bombarded with violence not only increases the probability that they might perform violent acts themselves but perhaps just as serious, reduces normal compassion for victims of aggression and violence.[36] In the Book of Proverbs, there is a description of a generation that frightens me:

There is a generation, whose teeth are as swords, and their jaw teeth as knives, to devour the poor from off the earth, and the needy from among men.

Proverbs 30:14 KJV

I can't help but wonder how much more accurate a picture could be presented of the children now growing up in our homes, nurtured on violence from Bugs Bunny to the National Hockey League.

Just as serious as the threat of a more violent generation is the problem that excessive TV violence is creating a climate of fear. "Watching television," says a researcher, "teaches people not only how to be violent, but also how to react to violence by passivity. In fact the most serious result of exposure is fear. Fear causes people to stay home and watch television. Then the crime and violence shown on television increases their fear of the outside world—the classic self-perpetuation cycle of addiction." [37]

3. Passivity and fatigue. More and more writers now are noting the effects on children of the extended periods of passive watching. TV time is not *doing* time. It is just sit-and-stare time. In one inner-city enrichment program, child-care workers found they actually had to teach the preschoolers they worked with how to walk and run. The children had spent days and days of early childhood under the baby-sitting care of television, and were physically incapable of performing even the most normal functions. Even an hour and a half of television can turn active children into staring zombies. And, of course, this very anesthetizing effect is what makes television so popular with parents who find in television the reprieve from parenthood once supplied by grandparents who would take the children over for an hour or so a day.

It is now generally agreed that television produces bored kids, kids who find the normal classroom insufferably dull by comparison with electronic education, kids who want to be entertained rather than instructed or trained. Even a program as excellent in content as the Canadian "Mr. Dressup" conveys the impression that somewhere there exist adults whose sole purpose in life is to entertain boys and girls. This role a normal parent cannot fill.

Children who are naturally creative and naturally active are being robbed of the time and initiative to "do."

Another way in which television is robbing children of their health is by encroaching on sleep time. It is easy to let TV-numbed children sit up late. In a grade-five classroom where I was teaching, 80 percent of the children stayed up to watch the late-night (midnight to two o'clock) Thursday-night movie. Little wonder they couldn't think! And this finding could be verified by many other teachers. Even in homes where children do not sit up to extreme hours, bedtimes are often set to accommodate the TV schedule rather than to reflect the child's real needs for adequate rest. The poor performance of many children, their irritable behavior, and general apathy can be traced quite simply to poor rest patterns developed by the home in response to the TV schedule.

4. Courtesy, conversation, and self-discipline. Because television absorbs children into a selfish, personalized experience, children are less quarrelsome and less demanding while they are watching television. But, at the same time, they are failing to learn the disciplines of courtesy, of making interesting and enjoyable conversation, of relating effectively to their siblings and parents. Parents who allow television to dominate their children's leisure time may not even realize the need for training in these disciplines. But parents who have removed the television as a dominant force will know that, over and above the obvious corrupting or harmful effects of current television, the very act of television watching interrupts normal behavior.

In her book *The Plug-In Drug,* author Marie Winn says:

> The developing child needs opportunities to work out his basic family relationships. The television experience only reduces these opportunities. The child needs to develop self-direction, to liberate himself from dependency. The television experience helps to perpetuate dependency. The television experience is at best irrelevant and at worst detrimental to children's needs." [38]

5. The capacity to believe. Television brings highly realistic fiction into children's lives so early that children are easily confused. Many tears have been shed in our living room as young children empathize with an endangered character, whether an animal on the "Wonderful World of Disney" or the poor old carpenter in "Pinocchio." Learning to distinguish between reality and fantasy is basic to coping with life. As the children mature they can understand that the hero isn't actually in danger. But young children may not be able to cope with such realistic fantasy.

Television can be deceiving. How many young children have asked, "Can Mister Rogers see me? I waved to him and he didn't wave back." Gradually the little one becomes aware of television's illusions and lays aside his early-childhood belief. The danger is that in the process he may lay aside true beliefs as well.

"Mr. Dressup" opens a world of music, art, and imaginative play. One day, after watching the show, my five-year-old nephew observed to his mother, "Mr. Dressup and Jesus are just the same, aren't they?"

"What do you mean?" his mother asked, startled by the comparison.

"Well, they both do miracles, don't they?" The similarity was obvious to the child, who daily watched the magic of the children's entertainer, and daily heard of the miracles of Jesus. Unaware of the technical devices which create the TV illusions, he was convinced that Mr. Dressup actually performed miracles.

Naturally, as the child grows older, he discovers that he has been tricked by lights and lenses. And he concludes that Mr. Dressup does not do miracles at all. What does he then decide about his belief in the miracles of Jesus? That they were merely tricks? Children who lay aside one illusion after another may develop an unhealthy skepticism toward all they hear and see.

Commercials pose perhaps the biggest threat to a child's credulity. Many spokesmen outside of Christian circles have noted the effect of misleading commercials. While adults may have learned to assume that most commercials are overstatements, children are much more vulnerable. They believe what they see.

Pamela Sigurdson, chairwoman of a committee studying children's commercials, stated on the Canadian Broadcasting Corporation National News (June 12, 1973): "The abuse of children's credulity by commercials destroys children's ability to believe anything said by adults." An article in *Today's Health* cites a Harvard study of TV ads: "As a result of TV sales pitches, children are becoming cynical and distrustful and the attitudes they develop in reaction to television carry over into other experiences." [39]

Some TV programs carry frontal attacks on the Christian faith. Nontheistic theories dominate science programs. Witches and seances become humorous, everyday fare. And TV dramas stereotype the hypocritical churchgoer, the effeminate minister, or the carping Christian woman. I consider this antisupernatural bias and scoffing at the believer threatening to children's confidence in Christ.

Children who become TV skeptics may well come to wonder what can be trusted. We must work to preserve our children's willingness to trust, for personal Christianity is based upon the ability to believe. Our Lord expressed His view of an adult responsibility to children: "It were better for him that a millstone were hanged about his neck, and he cast into the sea, than that he should offend one of these little ones" (Luke 17:2 KJV).

The ability to believe is one of God's best gifts to children, and we must not allow TV to destroy it. Our prime task is to prepare our children for that act of faith which brings them into a personal relationship with the Lord Jesus.

What can a Christian parent do? We do live in the electronic age and our children do view a great deal of television, some good and some bad. Shall we throw away our TV sets? Certainly that is one answer. And perhaps if we cannot assume the responsibility of control, it would be the best answer. But it is a negative one. I feel our responsibility is to help children draw the distinctions which TV often blurs.

First of all, youngsters need to distinguish between *reality and fantasy*. Fantasy, of course, is not intrinsically wrong. But it must be clearly separated from reality.

Children also need to learn to distinguish between *truth and lies*. Parents can point out misleading phrases in television commercials. They can explain how camera techniques make a toy look far more attractive than it is in actual life. I hear my older children explaining to the younger ones, "Don't get too excited about that doll. It's not that great."

Finally, children need to distinguish between *God's truth and*

TV's errors. Young children who cannot make this distinction should simply be prevented from watching misleading programs. An older child with a firm foundation of Bible truth might view some of these programs with his parents. A discussion time afterward will help him become aware of truth and error.

Because we want to safeguard our children's minds and health and faith, we are taking several steps in our home to control TV viewing.

We monitor children's television. Television is easily censored. Each set has an "off" button. We use ours! Children should not be responsible for selecting their own programs. Some are virtually hypnotized by TV and cannot bring themselves to turn it off.

We select educational programs, entertaining fantasies, violence-free cartoons (if we can find them), and informative nature programs to enrich our children's minds. Such selectivity, of course, means the TV cannot be used as an unpaid baby-sitter, tempting as that sometimes is.

We discipline our own TV viewing so our children are not exposed to unsuitable programs for them, or learning from our viewing patterns that "anything is okay for adults." Paul said, "If food causes my brother to stumble, I will never eat meat again . . ." (1 Corinthians 8:13 NAS). We should be able to say, "If that program could cause my child to stumble, I will not watch it."

We restrict the number of hours our children watch, remembering that the hours spent in front of the TV are passive, nondoing hours, and hours spent in a fantasy world. As a mother I have been amazed at my children's sudden flowering of creativity and purposeful play patterns when the TV is out for repairs. Our children need time to play, to create, to read, to practice their music lessons. We feel that one hour per day of carefully selected television is a maximum for any member of our family, including the little tots. And as our children grow—into club activities, sports, and music lessons—we find they have less and less time for TV.

Our TV is a small set that slips under an end table unless in use. Its physical attractiveness is minimal as we strive to underplay the natural attractiveness of synchronized motion and sound. Some people demote their TV from the living room to a family room. Here, however, children often have even more access to unmonitored television programing. Our family room is dominated by musical instruments, and the children watch almost no television that we do not watch with them—"Sesame Street" excepted.

When we first pared the TV schedule to its extreme spareness, the children complained. Now they wonder how their friends find time for TV. "You know what Dick said to me today?" Geoff came home to tell one day.

"No," I said. "What?"

"He said, 'Your family has so much fun. You're always doing something. All we ever do is sit around and watch TV.' "

If we are to prevent TV from doing irreparable damage, we must be honest with children—utterly, transparently honest. In contrast to the media which batter our children's minds with half-truths and misleading advertisements, Christian adults must be totally truthful. If we want our youngsters to believe what we tell them about Jesus Christ, our Saviour, we must give honest, direct answers to all our children's questions. We owe them these honest answers.

We need to draw a clear distinction between the authenticity of Bible stories and illusions of TV fiction. From earliest childhood, children need to be clearly taught the difference between fact and fiction. "Did it *really* happen?" our young ones ask time and time again. In this way they learn to distinguish between reality and fantasy.

Parents can take time to explain to young children that what they are viewing is make-believe. Even preschoolers can understand a clear explanation of basic camera techniques that fool the eye. A visit to a TV station to watch a show being produced helps children understand the relation of actor to camera, and camera to viewer.

"Once upon a time" can become a key to the golden door of fantasy—one which we should open often with our children. But, opening the Word of God should signal to them that we are dealing with historical and eternal truths. If such clear distinctions are taught, then when our children ask, "Did Jesus *really* do that?" the affirmation we give is a real and acceptable endorsement.

Above all, we need to expose children to God's Word. Perhaps one of the most disturbing statistics turned up by the Zuck and Getz study of Christian youth is that, while Christian young people watched just about as much TV as their non-Christian peers, few teens said their families have family devotions every day, and only a fourth of the teens read the Bible daily.[40]

"Faith cometh by hearing, and hearing by the word of God" (Romans 10:17 KJV). By reading the Scriptures with their child, parents can activate his God-given ability to believe. We can keep our children from being squeezed into conformity with the values of the world. The Lord Jesus Himself provided the prescription: "I pray not that thou shouldest take them out of the world," He petitioned concerning His disciples, "but that thou shouldest keep them from the evil . . . . Sanctify them through thy truth: thy word is truth" (John 17:15, 17 KJV). By contrast with the muddy grays in the wasteland of TV, "Every word of God is pure" (Proverbs 30:5 KJV). The Bible can help clear befuddled thinking.

Uncontrolled television can debilitate our children's ability to exercise saving faith. We must counter this influence with disciplined control and with daily exposure to that great tool of discernment, God's Word. If we read the Bible to our children daily, discussing its truth with them and living out its guidelines, we give them a standard of truth by which they may judge all of their world. The Scriptures are still able to make our children, as they made young Timothy, "wise unto salvation through faith which is in Christ Jesus" (2 Timothy 3:15 KJV).

12

Body Truth

We are looking forward to having children with sane, balanced, healthy and happy attitudes toward sex.

I was "great with child." My three-year-old son and my two-year-old daughter were fascinated. The first question was, "How come you're getting so fat, Mommy?" There was excitement when they learned there was a new baby growing inside me. The children would sit on either side of me and place their hands on my abdomen to feel the baby move inside my womb. The little unborn one was very much a part of the family long before her birth. By the time I was pregnant with Mitchell, the two older children were more sophisticated in their questions: "How does the baby grow inside Mother?" "Doesn't it get mixed up with your dinner down there?" "How will the baby get out?" And of course the question, "But how does the baby start growing there?"

It is very natural for children to learn the basic facts of sexual reproduction through the additional pregnancies and births in the family. With today's small families, however, this opportunity is not as readily available as it was to larger families. But whatever stimulus starts the question-and-answer process, sex education begins at home.

"Letting it all hang out" is the mode of sex education today. Educators insist on telling everybody at any age anything they may have wanted to know about sex but hadn't even thought of asking. Since the schools are increasingly encroaching in this area, and the media are explicit, a sound, value-shaped understanding of sex must be given to children at an early age. Children should go to school knowing about the difference between the sexes and the basics of human reproduction. If that sounds like too stiff a curriculum, remember that it will be covered in detail in the washroom, if not in the classroom, as soon as the kids get to school.

How do we go about teaching our children about sex? We need to remember, first of all, that attitudes will be at least as important as words. Perhaps it would be a good idea to take the title off the project of "sex education" and realize that teaching our children about sex is just a part of teaching them about themselves, about their bodies, and about their world. How we go about it will color their self-acceptance and their approach to sexuality as they mature. The adult parent who interacts with the child on matters of sex needs to be frank and accepting of the child's interest as being something which is normal and natural. He should be frank in his answers, but not too explicit in detail. At the same time, the whole field of sexual inquiry should be treated as something that is private, something to be discussed with the parents in confidence. This is necessary to prevent the child from being too blunt or frank in his own disclosures, with a resulting embarrassed response from other children or adults. It is also part of modesty training. A child who asks a specific sexual question in a public place could be told, "We'll talk about it when we get home." For example, a child who encounters animal mating at a zoo could be encouraged to observe unobtrusively with discussion and explanation to follow at home and in private.

Because of the emotion-charged field we enter when we begin to discuss sex with our children, the choice of words is also important. Today the trend is to use precise medical terminology. This is in keeping with the practice of never talking down to children. There are no better words for describing body parts than their physiological names. Technical terms are a little less emotionally charged than many of the diminutives or euphemisms which have been developed for describing genitalia or sexual activities. Vulgar terms are clearly inappropriate. But even the most accurate and articulate parents may find that their terms of instruction are translated into "childese." Parents may find their son referring to his "peanuts," or their daughter aware of her "velvet"—despite the fact that the correct terms have been used by the parents. Because the child looks for ways to associate the words he hears with the environment as he knows it, technical terms may not always have the same precision for a child as they do for an adult.

Thinking ahead of the words and the way in which children's questions can be answered in clear but not overly explicit phrasing is worth the parents' time. Naturally the basic "how" of teaching children about sex is the same as the basic methodology for teaching our children anything in their preschool and early-childhood years. That is simply to answer the child's questions in as crisp and clear a way as possible. This approach also solves the "when" of sex education. The child's own interest and curiosity in this subject is the natural pacer for deciding upon the timing for introducing sexual concepts to the child. At the same time, the parent may need to be alert to opportunities that are presenting themselves without the child's awareness. Thus when a child comments on a friend's pregnancy by noting that she's wearing a loose dress, or that she "sure is getting fat these days," the parent should not leave the situation unexplained.

In one seminar I was conducting, I was asked, "What do you do about the child who doesn't ask any questions?" This poses a unique problem and perhaps it happens most often in a home where the child is the youngest in the family, and therefore does not observe his mother experiencing pregnancy. The child who does not ask questions should be stimulated to think about human reproduction. Stimuli that could be used within the home would be such things as a pair of mating animals. Guinea pigs will go through the whole process of mammalian breeding and gestation and birth, and give a child a good introduction to the basics. Used along with the book *Susie's Babies,* this can be a good introduction to reproduction.[41]

There are some good books which can be used within the home as a storybook introduction to the basic facts of procreation and of birth. One of these is *I Wonder, I Wonder.*[42] This has been a favorite with our children. Starting from the question "Where did I come from?" the Childcraft Supplement book *About Me* gives a clear, well-illustrated explanation.[43]

Because there are so many books available on the market today, parents should review material with care to be sure that the content is Christian in outlook and in presentation. That may sound like a needless quibble, for Christian anatomy and non-Christian anatomy are not distinguishable. But a Christian attitude toward sex is distinctive, and book material should (1) represent the body as something worthy of reverent respect; (2) represent the process of procreation and birth as God's plan for human reproduction; and (3) keep the whole matter of sexual interaction firmly placed within the context of marriage and the family. These basic understandings are lacking in many secular productions for teaching children the facts about sex. Christian parents need to be wary, for sex education cannot be separated from values. Help is available from Christian publishers. The Family Life series from Concordia comes complete with a parent's guide which covers basic attitudes and the ways in which these can be taught within a family setting at various ages.[44] Other book materials are available.

What, then, are the basic understandings which we would want to teach our children prior to their reaching school age?

Understanding #1: Our bodies are wonderful and made by God. I like my body. Before there can be any happy married sexuality, there must be a basic appreciation of one's own sex, and a basic acceptance of one's own body. The Christian faith has always repudiated gnosticism as a heresy. The concept that the body is evil and only the spirit good and acceptable to God is *not* a Christian one. God is the designer, creator, and the sustainer of human physical existence, and this needs to color all that we say about sexuality. We have already talked about children's acceptance of their bodies as preliminary to self-acceptance. It is also preliminary to sexual adjustment.

Understanding #2: Boys' and girls' bodies differ. Those differences constitute "sex." Within a family of mixed-sex siblings, children will early notice the distinguishing features between boys' and girls' bodies. It is very natural for children of close ages to bathe together in preschool years. And nothing could be more natural than their discovery of their genital differences in this kind of setting. By the time the children are of school age, bath-time exposure to a sibling of the opposite sex should be over. The basic understandings have been reached, and now there should be an emphasis on modesty and privacy.

Modesty training can enter a child's experience from perhaps the age of three forward. After toilet training is accomplished, a gradual development of modesty should occur, beginning with being covered in front of strangers, and keeping nakedness within the family unit; progressing to nakedness only within the closed doors of the bathroom or bedroom during the bath or dressing period; and by the age of four and a half to five (perhaps best determined by the time at which children begin to joke about each other's differences, or to be embarrassed by each other's nudity), separation of the sexes for bath and sleeping time.

Modesty within the family unit seems to me a wise way to lay foundations for self-respect and chastity. Family life should include modesty between the sexes and personal privacy.

Children will have some encounter with the parent of the same sex in nude or near-nude situations: when changing for swimming, for example, or sharing a bathroom. This is incidental to life and part of life. But the new casualness about family nudity, exemplified by "family bathrooms," can only serve to confuse children concerning both modesty and their own emotional responses.[45] Children's curiosity about the adult body can be satisified by exposure to nonerotic and nonprovocative material: classical art or photographs in the *National Geographic* would serve this purpose.

"Family-life education" has become, in many cases, a cover for voyeuristic film and literature. Parents are wise to insist on previewing materials proposed for presentation to their preschool children.

Children should not be offered more detail than is necessary to answer their questions. The child who insists, "But *how* does Daddy start the baby in Mummy?" can be given a factual answer, or simply told to wait until he is old enough to understand. The little girl whose response to her mother's explanations was a wrinkled nose and, "Oh, Mom! Did you and Daddy have to do that?" is not unusual when the facts are too explicit for a child.

Another area in which wisdom and caution need to be exercised is in the area of hugging and fondling. A tiny child cannot be overhugged, of course. As they grow up through their preschool years, boys and girls alike need to experience the hugging of both parents, the physical closeness and warmth that is the basic preparation for adult sexuality later. However, modesty and discretion need to be developed. After infancy, children should not be encouraged to feel their mothers' breasts. There will be a natural curiosity expressed at some point in attempts to feel or to fondle. The mother should push the exploring hands away, saying, "That's private for Mommy. It embarrasses me when you touch." [Similarly, parents need to express that there are portions of the male body that children may not explore with their hands—or in other ways.] It will only be with this kind of training that a child will learn to respect the private and sexual portions of the body of a person of the opposite sex.

What do we, as parents, hope to achieve by carefully undergirding our children's knowledge of sexuality with teaching in the home? We are looking forward to having children with sane, balanced, healthy and happy attitudes toward sex. Children who accept and respect their own bodies as God's plan and design. Children with enough information concerning the opposite sex to prevent morbid or furtive curiosity from developing. Children who recognize that sex is an area of human behavior that is governed by sacred rules. We can look forward to adolescents who accept puberty as part of God's design in their lives and who approach sexual maturity with confidence and with sound character displayed in self-respect, self-discipline, and responsibility. Ultimately, we look forward to their becoming adults who can move into the sexual relationship of marriage with minds unclouded by guilt, with a healthy appreciation of God's plan and purpose in human sexuality, with a happy acceptance of sex as a normal part of adult life within marriage, and with anticipation of the whole wonderful process of procreation by which they will bring another generation into the world.

Part III

CREATIVITY

Human creativity . . . is finding new ways of putting existing components together . . . . God has planted the creative potential within our children. It is our duty—and what a joyous one—to let that creativity flourish in our homes.

The chapters that follow explore ways in which parents can stimulate, facilitate, and respond to the creative impulse within their preschool children.

13

Creativity Begins at Home

Your response to your child's efforts will be the greatest stimulus you could possibly make to more creative effort on his part.

My left-handed two-year-old had finally figured out how to use the kindergarten scissors. She sat, busily cutting, in the middle of a pile of slivered scraps of yellow paper. "Cammie-Lou," I encouraged, "you've learned how to cut. That's wonderful!" I gave her a little hug, and then, with a sinking sense of recognition, picked up one of the little bits of paper. Cammie had just shredded the crucial second draft of one of my first manuscripts. Encouraging creativity at home has always had its hazards. But the rewards outweigh the problems.

Along with the word *love, creativity* is one of the most overused words of our day. Everything's coming up creative—especially high-priced toys. It's the catchword on a half dozen psychologies and a baker's dozen of religious innovations. I am not all that wild about creativity if all it means is doing something different every day. But I am deeply interested in the native creativity of children—a creativity that has brightened my life for the past ten years.

Human creativity—the kind of creativity that is needed desperately now in all of the arts and sciences and technologies—is finding new ways of putting existing components together to make a whole. That's all. The child who turns the laundry basket upside down over himself (preferably when it is empty) and becomes a fearsome lion in the zoo is being creative. He has seen another way of composing the components to make a new configuration. The child who takes a cardboard box and with flow pen, glue, and imagination converts it into a car or a stove or a television set is being creative. The child who sits at a typewriter and

117

composes a letter to his grandmother is being creative.

Creativity is something which develops through a number of phases as the preschool child grows. (All of the phases I delineate are overlapping, of course, with gradual shading into the next phase. And the ages I suggest are only rough estimates based on my own observations.)

From age six months to one year, the child's creativity is mostly seen in manipulating his own body or the immediate things he uses: playing with his hands; finding new ways to pull himself to a stand; learning to retrieve his bottle. From one to three years, creativity takes two main forms: creative use of words to manipulate the environment, and imaginative play. Children's early free-art forms reach their peak during the fourth year. Then a sense of representationalism sets in—a desire to make the picture conform to the thing—and the free drawing of happy faces or brightly colored circles gives way to more difficult and less frequently successful attempts to draw representationally.

At about age five, children become interested in crafting things: making candles, cookies, wall hangings. You name it, they'll make it. Their interest switches from art for art's sake to craft for function's sake. This tendency grows with the child. At about six years of age, the compulsion to make things that are real, working, and functional seems to reach its early peak. The pleasure Mitchell got one day from cutting a piece of plywood to a size I needed for fixing a magazine rack was greater than the pleasure he now gets out of drawing a picture. He wants what he is making to be functional—a difficult desire to bring to realization in our technological era.[46]

The parental role in the face of this natural outpouring of childhood creativity is fourfold: (1) to *recognize* developing creative abilities; (2) to *stimulate* creativity; (3) to *facilitate* the child's imaginative projects; and (4) to *respond* to the child's products. Like the "Competence-Confidence Cycle," this, too, is essentially circular, since response in turn stimulates further creativity (Figure 2).

1. Recognize developing creative abilities. "Oh, my, you have such talented children," one mother sighs to another.

"What a talented family," another comments.

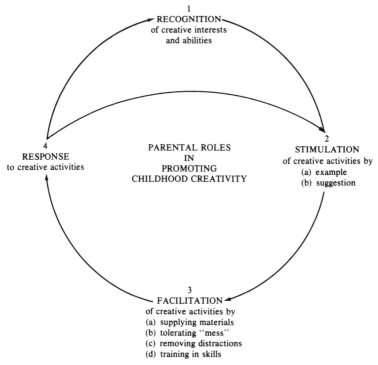

Figure 2. Creativity Cycle.

And in Christian circles, we have become so sensitive about the words *gifts* and *talents* that we are not sure whether we should be complimented or reproached. The idea has been communicated that "gifts" given by the Holy Spirit are entirely different from native abilities or learned skills because they are entirely supernatural. However, a close study of the Word of God reveals that this is not necessarily so. And understanding how gifts and talents relate to each other is important if we are to place a value on ascertaining our children's talents and giving opportunities for their development.

A case study to consider is the young man Timothy. Paul speaks to Timothy about the responsible use of a gift: ". . . kindle afresh the gift of God which is in you through the laying on of my hands" (2 Timothy 1:6 NAS). But, before Paul ever laid eyes, lèt alone hands, on Timothy, there was considerable preparation.

In 2 Timothy 1:5, we find that the faith had been lived out before him by his mother and his grandmother. In 2 Timothy 3:14, 15, we learn that the Word of God had been carefully and soundly taught to him. In Acts 16:1, 2, we find that he was using this background plus native leadership ability to build a sound reputation for Christian living and leadership among the brethren. So, when Paul laid his hands on Timothy and the Holy Spirit endowed him with a special gift for the ministry, he was confirming and empowering a set of natural abilities and carefully taught behaviors.

Or, if you wish, look at Paul. We learn that God separated Paul to Himself from birth (Galatians 1:15). When Ananias laid hands on Paul to ordain him for the service to which God had set him apart, the zeal was already there (Acts 9:17). The training in Old Testament Scriptures was already there. The native leadership ability was already there. The education and training was already there. And God, by His Holy Spirit, took hold of this many-talented man and filled him, and made all that knowledge and zeal and training and ability a gift to His Body, the Church.

Doesn't this make the childhood years exciting and interesting? Instead of waiting passively with the idea that God will someday drop a gift on your children, you recognize that God had His hand on each child from before birth. Genes and chromosomes are just as surely counted as the hairs of the head. Your child is equipped with the potential necessary for his part in God's program.

How, practically, do we discover our children's abilities? And how do we help prepare them for use in God's work?

(a) Watch your children. There is no substitute for really knowing your children. What activities do they most often choose to do, given a free choice? A two-year-old I know already loves to take apart and put together Lego blocks. She has an interest in building and in putting things together, which suggests a mechanical bent. It will be interesting to watch it develop. "Having then gifts differing . . ." is an apparent condition even when children are very young (Romans 12:6 KJV). It takes time spent really seeing your children. It takes supportive encouragement together with noncontrolling interest in their activities to really discover what they like to do.

(b) Be supportive of all natural abilities. Do not be more supportive of artistic bents than of mechanical ones; more interested in a flair for math than a flair for poetry. Give all abilities your enthusiastic encouragement. Don't narrow the channel on your child. If he shows a flair in some area, encourage it. But do not act as though that is the only ability the child has. Encourage breadth of development. Your children may well be ten-talent people if you give them a chance to discover all of their abilities. Don't assume that your talents will be your children's—or insist that they should be. But be aware of hereditary possibilities and cultivate interests as your children show them.

(c) Accept development and change. Don't be surprised if a natural artistic flair seems to dry up. Recognize that if there is strong artistic talent it will flourish again. Keep opening doors in as many directions as you can, at the same time giving thorough training in at least one area of ability for several years.

(d) Don't wait until you see a big talent to offer training. Many parents say, "Well, we'll let Johnny start piano lessons, and if he shows a talent, we'll let him keep at it." That is really not good enough. Johnny may not mature into his ability for several years. Or he may not have a great deal of natural ability, but with training may gain a very worthwhile skill as well as the discipline of practice.[47] When we started Geoffrey on piano lessons at age five, we wondered if perhaps he was tone deaf. He had never sung the songs at Sunday school. In fact, he seemed quite disinterested in vocal music. But music lessons were available, and we felt he would enjoy a music ability in his adult years. Now, to our great delight and considerable surprise, Geoffrey is displaying a talent and promise in music that is exciting.

2. Stimulate. In the early stages, the best stimulation to creativity is to enter into imaginative play with children; to help them unlock their world with words; to praise their innovative play or art. Supplying toys and helping the child see or create in new ways may be important, but need not be expensive. Looking at and reading books together and going for walks help to stimulate the child to *see*—and that is absolutely basic to creativity. "Originality," said Woodrow Wilson, "is simply a fresh pair of eyes." Those eyes the child has; you can help him to see in new ways.

Suggesting activities will be a part of your parental role as stimulator.

The greatest stimulus of all will be parents who value "doing" and "being" above "having." Such a parental attitude will be reflected in creative children.

3. Facilitate. You facilitate your child's creativity by following up the child's choice of activity and making it possible. You may have to say, "We don't have those materials, but what we can substitute is . . . ." You may have to say, "That would need too much help and I'm busy this morning, but you do something else and we'll work on that project this afternoon." You should encourage children to projects which need a minimum of your supervision and help. Complicated crafts which require endless adult intervention are not for preschoolers. Avoid them. Children's sense of self-worth is enhanced by the "I can do it myself" feeling.

You will facilitate creativity by supplying materials and a work space suitable to the child's projects. You may have to take a few minutes to help the child round up essential materials or decide upon satisfactory substitutes—another creative activity—but time spent in finding the crayons and glue and paper is repaid in a period of meaningful activity.

Facilitating includes developing an attitude of tolerance toward the "mess" which goes with children's doings. I recall a housekeeper who worked for me for two days while I substitute taught. I came home to find the house shining and the children neat and tidy. I thought she was a dream come true—until my four-year-old told me how the day had gone. "After lunch, she put away all our toys and crayons and things and made us watch TV. She wouldn't let me have scissors or anything! She said, 'That would make a mess.' " Such an attitude was foreign to our kids who were allowed to use the kitchen or living room for their many projects with only two conditions. One was that they cleaned up one activity before embarking on another. The other was that, when the day's end came, they helped with a complete pickup.

Facilitating may also include removing some distractions: turning off the TV, sending neighbor kids home, putting baby in bed or playpen. And, of course, as the child matures, facilitating means taking the time to teach the necessary skills for increasingly interesting creative design.

While you go about your work, you may have to stop to help a child with a problem in his project, to answer a question, to spell a word (or a dozen of them), to untangle a knotted thread. All are worth your time. Your interest and time will bear fruit in your child's creative flowering.

4. *Respond.* The child brings you the finished project. It doesn't resemble the item shown in the craft book. Be glad. Glue is dripping from the sheet. Wipe it up quickly. But note the boldness, the freshness of color, or just a sincerity of effort—well worth your encouragement and praise!

Respond with genuine interest: "How did you make the tree look so old?" With questions concerning content: "Why does the little girl look so sad?" With praise, always: "Your picture is lovely," or "That was a hard project and you felt like quitting. But don't you feel good now that it's done?" Respond with encouragement. "That's so nice that I think you should do another one." Respond with display: "Let's hang this picture right here where our friends can see it, too." Respond with use: "I like that card so much I'm going to send it to Grandma for her birthday." Respond with delight: "I would never have seen it that way. What an interesting picture."

Do not hold up unreasonable standards. Judge your child's work as a child's work, and don't let perfectionism become the stumbling block to his growth. Encourage sincerity, effort, originality, beauty, or interest.

Your response to your child's efforts will be the greatest stimulus you could possibly make to more creative effort on his part. Your enthusiasm builds your child's confidence in his own creative work. Whether or not your child becomes an artist or a writer or a poet is beside the point. We need more creative housewives and more creative bank managers. We need, desperately, people who can see new ways of approaching old and difficult problems in society as a whole. We need creative Christians. God has planted the creative potential within our children. It is our duty—and what a joyous one—to let that creativity flourish in our homes.

14

Creativity and Play

From the two basic elements of imagination and physical props, a child makes his creative play.

I find a verse sketch in an old notebook:

> Cammie-Lou is serving tea
> Every day at half-past three.
>
> First she spreads a tiny tea cloth
> Then she sets her dishes out.
> Now she's calling, "Tea is ready!"
> Geoff, come quickly, or she'll pout.
>
> Carefully she fills the teacups
> From her teapot, to the brim.
> Now she passes out the cookies:
> "Two for you and two for him."
>
> Tea today with Cammie-Lou,
> Little lady, half-past two.

The ritual of serving tea exemplifies creative play. The elements: a child's imagination and some simple props. The activities: manipulation of the props and interaction with other people. Let's take a closer look at "child's play."

Elements of Creative Play

Anybody who has really observed children at play knows that there's nothing simple about child's play. The elements which make up the naturally creative play of children are simple, but they are used in a variety of amazingly complex ways by even very young children. The basic elements of child's play are (1) the

125

imagination and intelligence of the child, and (2) the "props" or material things which occur in his world. Using his imagination and intelligence, the child manipulates the props in various ways. His play may be enriched by interaction with other imaginative humans—child or adult.

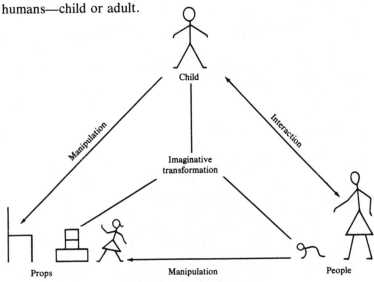

Figure 3. Child's Play.

Imagination is the ability to see something that does not in actual material reality exist. It is a gift that keeps the world young. It is the gift of writers such as C. S. Lewis and J. R. R. Tolkien. And it is God's gift to every little child. There is an evidence of damage being done to children's capacity to imagine by the continuous flow of explicitly pictorial material in the form of television programing. But children who are not overexposed to television will exhibit a marvelous facility for seeing not only with their eyes but also with their minds. I have a six-year-old who is not at all concerned if a book has no pictures. "Read me the story and I will make the pictures inside my head," he says. It is the ability to make pictures, friends, and worlds in one's mind that we call imagination. It is, by extension, the ability to make a transformation between what a thing is, normally and functionally, and what the child wishes to represent in his play.

Even before children are able to speak clearly they reveal their ability to imagine. A toddler barely a year old may come to his mother with his tiny fist clenched and ceremoniously offer her a "candy." When the mother holds her hand cuplike and receives the fantasy gift, she delights the child, for she shares, momentarily, in his fantasy.

"Let's pretend. Let's pretend that this chair is a throne, and you are the princess," and away children go, creating a fairy world in their imaginations. I remember being overwhelmed at a child's capacity for abstract imaginativeness when Heather Ruth at four said, "I wish I had two buttons on this chair. I would push one button to make the time go fast when the day is boring, and the other button to make the time go slow when the day is fun."

The role of parents with regard to imagination is just the same as with regard to any other element of creativity—that is, to be aware of it and to stimulate it by entering into "Let's imagine" games. "Let's shut our eyes and pretend we are at Grandma's house," is a starter. But, of course, most often the parents will not have to start this kind of game. When it comes to imagination, "A little child shall lead" (Isaiah 11:6 KJV).

I remember Mitchell saying to me, "I wish that I could just dial the phone and when Grandma said hello I could slide out of the phone and be in her house." The idea of material transfer had popped into the mind of a four-year-old. Together we chatted about what it would be like if he could zip rapidly through the telephone wire and emerge at the other end of the receiver in his grandma's house. How surprised Grandma would be—and what fun it would be! But it couldn't be more fun than the lunchtime we spent discussing it.

Any parent who considers an imaginative excursion fun and who responds with enthusiasm, entering the child's imagined concept with him, will be, by that response, also facilitating and stimulating his child's basic drive to imaginative and creative play.

The second element of child's play is "properties"—in the stage sense of the word—the material items a child will manipulate as a part of his creative play. These are of all kinds. There are the props which exist in the environment of the child. The toilet bowl becomes an exciting and exotic fish pond at least once. The bathtub is an ocean in which fleets of ships have been sailed, while little boys have forgotten that they had necks and elbows to clean. Kitchen chairs become trains, buses, planes. Or they can be turned upside down and draped with blankets to create tiny tents. Kitchen tables, too, provide play space. For her children, my sister, Marg, took an old sheet and cut windows and a door in it. This sheet could be draped over a table and immediately the area under it would be a playhouse for her children.

But, of course, there are also the "found props" for children's play—the extra things that children find all around them which they can use for fun. And I suppose at the top of the list here is the all-time favorite: cardboard boxes. These can be crawled into, pushed, pulled, sat on, and converted into dozens of things with a few lines of felt pen. Strips of corrugated cardboard can be turned into roads, scrub boards, or delightful rhythm-band instruments. Empty paper rollers from toilet paper or wax paper become an amazing array of things, from telescopes to flutes, in the hands of children. Bleach bottles become people, planters, doorstops. Plastic lids become stepping-stones or bases for indoor baseball. Any object that is nontoxic, unbreakable, and too big to swallow can be given to children to play with.

Then, of course, there are the bought props: toys. It is good to remember that everything marked "educational" isn't educational, that the age range marked on the side will be as variant as the child himself, and that one child's interests should not determine what you buy for another child. Some children are endlessly interested in manipulative toys such as building blocks, locking blocks, and mechanical sets of various kinds. Other children have limited interest in this kind of thing and prefer soft, cuddly toys. Child-powered toys will run a lot longer and get more creative use than battery or electrically powered toys. One has to be aware of the construction of toys, watching for sharp edges and removable parts. The single biggest rule about useful toys—toys which children enjoy—is that they are toys which a child can manipulate to create his own imaginative world. "Any child who has had a set of blocks cannot be said to have been deprived," someone has said. In our eagerness to supply more, we sometimes clog the toy boxes with junk. One good reason to limit children's television intake is to guard them from the relentless advertising of toys nobody needs but everybody has to have.

From the two basic elements of imagination and physical props, a child makes his creative play. He may or may not interact with other persons or with a pet or "pretend" playmate. Up to the age of three, children play happily by themselves, content to merely manipulate props. Only later do they seem eager for playmate interaction. The continuous drive in our society to put children into play groups, and our insistence that they become "socialized" early, sometimes amounts to a denial of the child's need for a time when he plays alone, finding his own identity, before he begins to share both himself and his toys.

With an expanded concept of "child's play," let's look at several modes of creative play.

Types of Creative Play

I flip through the photos I have collected through years of haphazard "mother photography." Round-cheeked children smile through clown paint; trail across the lawn in straggly parades; pose stiffly and shyly beside a favorite project; preen in a fancy dress. Picture after picture records a phase of family living already past for us, prompting memories more sharply focused than the photos, of four little children engaged in day after day of creative play. The categories of play which I describe here are those which I find best cover the varieties of play experiences which we recorded, with camera or pen, during those free wheeling preschool years with our children.

1. Tactile play. In tactile play the basic emphasis of the play is simply on feeling something different. This includes body play, water play, mud play—all the endless things children do for simple tactile pleasure. The development of tactile play into such things as sculpting figures, creating clay pots, or baking, is a gradual development of the child's normal delight in the sense of touch.

From playing with his own fingers and toes, the infant proceeds to reach out: for hair, or noses on other people. (Hearing a chuckle behind me in church one night, I turned quickly to see one-year-old Heather Ruth reaching with a hankie to wipe the

noses of the ladies in the pew behind us. Typical tactile play, and
creative at that—but I hastened to interrupt that game!) Later
comes water play: all kinds of wet, splashy fun. Building and
sculpting in sand, mud, or snow are other examples of tactile
play. Other materials supply other textures, other properties:
clay, Plasticine, Play-Doh, or actual bread or cookie dough.

Textural interest and enjoyment can be fostered by taking time
to *feel*. A quilt top with contrasting textures provides pleasant
bedtime exploration. A cloth book, with the pages formed of
various types of fabric, is fun for a touching-and-talking activity.
Collage making from a variety of materials is another extension of
tactile play.

2. *Manipulative play*. Here the emphasis is on the physical manipulation of props. The innumerable games that can be played
with building blocks, locking blocks, and various kinds of con-
structor sets fit in here. Pulling toys around is a special delight for
toddlers just after they learn to walk confidently. Some pull toys
not only follow the child obediently but also squawk, squeak,
rattle, or woof. Push toys, too, are a special pleasure for the
just-walking child. Besides the commercial push toys which may
shake, rattle, or roll, children will enjoy pushing all kinds of
"found props": their own strollers, the baby's carriage, the milk
glass right off the edge of the table . . . .

3. *Imitative play*. "Dress up" play is imitative play in its simplest
form—just for the fun of it. With closets full of clothes, from old
suits and formals to night wear, my friend Elsie Jones's home is a
favorite play spot for her grandchildren and my kids. They have
had happy hours of putting on costumes, traipsing downstairs to
be admired, photographed, and laughed at, then trudging back
upstairs to try on yet another outfit. Halloween is a cultural occa-
sion for indulging in dressing up just for fun. Because of the
lurking overtones of the occult, I avoid dressing my children as
witches or ghouls. But it is great fun for them to be swashbuckling
pirates, flirtatious senoritas, or snaggletoothed hobos—just for a
day. Perhaps of all the mental images that come to me of the
children playing, some of the most laughter filled are those of
dress-up days: children as funny, happy clowns, complete with

wide, red grins painted on their faces; the boys suddenly transformed into bashful and giggling girls in short-skirted dresses; and the girls turned into elegant ladies wobbling along on high-heeled shoes. Most parents could share memories of spontaneous dress-up fun. We recall the time Geoffrey opened the package from the mail-order house to discover a shiny new nylon snowsuit. He eagerly zipped himself into it, and then his four-year-old imagination made a sudden leap—and he saw himself as a spaceman. In just a few minutes he had found an empty cereal box to attach to his shoulders for an oxygen tank. Then, as his imagination filled in all the other details, he began springing around the living room, taking big, bouncy steps, emulating the first moon walk which he, as one of the very first of the space-age children, had watched so intently on TV a year or so before.

With or without dressing up, children take part in more complex imitative play in the form of dozens of kinds of role play. Some of the play is in imitation of adults with whom they have contact: everybody from doctors and nurses to policemen and preachers are "played back" by observant little children. And the parent who watches the playtime can learn a lot about how children see the adults around them. Usually just a few simple props are needed for each kind of role play: an inexpensive toy doctor's kit for clinic or hospital play; a blackboard and paper for endless rounds of playing school; paper and paper clips, a stapler, and a sheet of carbon paper for bustling and officious office work. Role play is almost always engaged in with interaction between two or more children. The fun lies in the sharing of the experience—and besides, the adult roles they are imitating almost always exist in interaction with others.

Part of the significance of imitative play lies in the identification of the child with significant adults in his life—most often, his parents. While both boys and girls engage in playing all kinds of imitative games, there is a persistent tendency to assume the role of the parent of the same sex as the child. The more flexible parents are in their own roles, the more widely the children will play identification-imitation games.

At yet another level of play, imitative play allows a child to enter, imaginatively, a role or experience which he has little ac-

cess to in any other way. Thus I have seen our children dress up
as little old ladies and men, leaning on canes and shuffling their
way along, hair powdered white with talcum and glasses perched
precariously on the end of gumdrop noses. They have enjoyed a
vicarious experience.

Each Christmas Eve while our children were preschoolers, we
helped them costume themselves in things easily found around
the house, to act out the story of the Christ's birth. The children
are gradually becoming too old to take this seriously. Geoffrey's
humorous asides robbed last Christmas's drama of its dignity, so
we will find some other way to enter into the Christmas experience this year.

Because imitative play is such an important part of childhood,
parents should seek ways to promote it. The parent who suggests,
"Why don't you play hospital? Here, I saved some empty pill
bottles for you," may trigger hours of role play. Inviting the children to act out their story from Sunday school rather than merely
telling it to you, or to set up a skit based on the day's Bible
reading, will stimulate imitative play. A closet or a trunk with old
clothes and the invitation to dress up will also facilitate and stimulate role play. Responding to imitative play is a must: not, "What
a mess!" or "Timmy, you go get that dress off right now, you're a
little boy," but, "Let's see now. Who are you today?" or "Let
me see if I can guess what story you're acting out." Keep the
camera handy to capture at least some of those parades and
charades for later pleasure.

4. Creating and using models of the real world. "Look," my five-
year-old nephew squealed. "There's a Cat exactly like mine."
We looked to see a huge Caterpillar tractor with its blade lowered,
moving dirt in a nearby lot. It was identical to the match-box
sized replica Terry held in his hand. "But," Terry added, "that
one is just big."

Children delight to play with or create models of the real world.
Many such models are made with meticulous detail by toy man-
ufacturers. Most children engage in their own creation of models,
as well. At age two or three, a child is satisfied if there is some
slight parallelism between his model and the real world. He does
not demand exactitude; he is only asking that the model be suffi-

ciently like its counterpart in the real world to allow him to manipulate it imaginatively. As children grow older they are looking for more sophisticated models: models which look like and/or function the same as their counterparts in the real world. At very early ages the children will create little model houses from cushions off the sofa. Cardboard boxes form the natural base for dozens of models—easy to make and free. It is an elementary way to get the extra use out of boxes that ecologists insist on, too. Here is a list of things our children have made from cardboard boxes—I'm sure your own additions would be endless.

Cardboard-Box Models:

(a) By simply sitting in a box big enough for one or two children: car; boat. These can be made to move by the child jerking himself forward. Fun—but tough on the wax job!

(b) By joining one or more sit-in boxes: train; bus; plane. Any transportation play can be made more fascinating by helping the children make a large roll of "scenery" by pasting pictures of scenes onto wide brown paper. One child can roll the scenery from one roller onto another, past the car, boat, train, etc., while the other children admire the view moving past them.

(3) By adding some details to the box with felt pen: inverted box becomes a kitchen range, with four burners drawn on top and an oven door either drawn or cut so that it opens; a more detailed vehicle, with headlights, etc.; a fireplace—an apple box with a cellophane cover is ideal, with flames drawn against the back inside of the box, or made to move like stick puppets, behind the cellophane cover; a playhouse can be made if a box big enough for the children to crawl into can be found—there are endless variations on this theme: children can cut windows and doors, add curtains, draw on shutters, flowers, shingles, add a chimney and cotton-batting smoke; a castle—either child scale, or smaller, depending on box size, complete with battlements and a drawstring bridge; mobile television camera made from a laundry-soap box, with the addition of one or more paper-roller lenses (ideal to take on a walk so that the child can "film" what he sees—when he gets home, he can draw the scenes he liked best and "show" his movie by rolling the drawings from one roller to the other); inverted box to serve as a table, desk, or bookcase.

5. Models built from other materials. Some models of the real world will combine the child's imagination with toys designed for this building, and such kits as Meccanno or Lego are good for children who enjoy manipulative toys. The creative child will be able to follow the kit's visual directions and then create his own variations with the same pieces. This is a prior step to model building of various kinds and increasing sophistication as the child grows older. As it becomes more sophisticated, model building may require carpentry skills. The parent who is willing to help the child saw a board or hold things together while the child pounds nails is not only courageous but also facilitating further creativity. Creating a miniature world is an extension of model making. A child with an electric train may add imaginative extras in the form of roadways, crossing markers, Plasticine people, and papier-mâché trees. Or a child may take a number of small toys, roughly matching in size, and, with empty cereal, macaroni, and hankie boxes, create a town.

My small spaceman who made himself into an astronaut by means of a snowsuit also created for himself a "moon station" which he equipped with all kinds of paraphernalia: bottles and lids and little tools, which to him seemed quite scientific. From this play place he had regular blast-offs during his third and fourth years.

Another kind of little world which a child may create is a world which incorporates his stuffed animals. My younger son has created zoos, camping expeditions, or just displays, using his many stuffed toys. One can go into his room sometimes and think of nothing more appropriate than "The Teddy Bears' Picnic" to describe the scene.

Another kind of little world which children may enjoy creating at a slightly more sophisticated stage is the creating of a terrarium. This can be in anything from a rose bowl right up to a large and properly regulated terrarium. Another kind of miniature world is the fishbowl or aquarium into which, as in the terrarium, miniature items can be put into place to create a kind of world. With both a terrarium and aquarium project, a large amount of parental help and supervision should be anticipated.

Creative play is as natural to the child as eating or sleeping.

Parental awareness and enthusiasm is the primary stimulus. Facilitation takes the form of supplying appropriate props. The response the child needs most is your interest and occasional participation. Remember, when you have a preschooler at home, it is still possible to slip "through the looking glass"!

15

Creativity and Crafts

Parents who take time out to teach skills, provide materials, and respond with enthusiasm, will help their children discover artistic talents and develop constructive pastimes.

It was a warm spring day when Mitchell ran into the house, excited and delighted, with a gray brown duck feather in his hand. He stroked it against his cheek as he felt its softness—the short feathers on one side and the long on the other forming their perfect striped pattern. "What can I make with it?" he asked.

We thought. "Well," I said, "the other kids used to make Indian headbands when they found a feather. They just took a piece of brown paper off the top of a bag and stapled the feather into it at the back. Then they decorated the band with Indian designs."

Mitchell shook his head. "No, I don't want to do that."

We thought again. "Well," I said, "did you know that at one time they used to use feathers such as this for pens?"

Now he was interested. His eyes lit up. "For pens? Could they really write with them?" he asked.

"Yes," I said, "but we've got a problem. We don't have any ink in the house."

We thought again. "I know," Mitchell said. "We could use some poster paint." And with that, a simple craft was under way. I took a knife and cut the quill off at an angle, then slit it up a little way so that it would hold the ink, while Mitch mixed up some paint to make "ink." For the next hour my four-year-old sat happily scratching away with a quill pen. Mitchell spent considerable time over the next several days using his quill pen for drawing, for printing, and just for enjoying the kind of scratchy sound it made.

The quill pen was just one of sudden "Let's make it" projects that have been a part of our children's experience at home. Some projects have been done with considerable facilitation and assistance from me; some have been completely spontaneous and done entirely by the children. I don't think I have ever said, "Well, children, shall we do a craft today?" Usually something we have done, something we have read, or some interesting object or material at hand has prompted us to launch into a creative project.

Crafts which children copy from a book are a pastime and teach children to follow directions. We can apply the word *creative* most accurately, however, to the child's unique bringing together of elements. His desire to create is as big as the child himself—particularly at the ages of four, five, and six. At four a tremendous drive to make interesting things appears as an early flowering of aesthetic impulses. By the age of five or six the child is more interested in making something which has a clearly defined social function as well as an aesthetic value. The more or less "pure" art forms develop first. First of these, of course, is drawing. From the child's diffuse scribbling from eighteen months to twenty-four months, there is, during the third year, a gradual expression of the child's desire to order and give form.

Stimulating the child's interest in drawing is not difficult. "Why don't you draw me a picture?" or "Draw what you saw on the way home," or "Draw how you feel this morning," or "Draw the way you think Grandma looks today." Sometimes, you could try listening to a recording—a classical piece such as Schumann's "Scenes From Childhood," or a piece of more modern music that deals in imitative harmony such as Ketelbey's "In a Chinese Temple Garden," or Saint-Saëns "Carnival of the Animals." Invite the child to draw what he imagines the music is about, or to express the way the music makes him feel.

Or you could let the painting or drawing stem out of a story time. "Would you like to draw something you saw in your mind while I was reading?" Some delightful preschool art was done by a handful of children I worked with using the song "I Know an Old Woman Who Swallowed a Fly." I sang the song for them and taught it to them. Then we acted out the song as we sang it, assuming each consumed animal's role in turn. After that, we spread out large sheets of white paper and I invited the children to draw the old lady in any way they wanted to. What delightful little old ladies those children drew, complete with spiders that were tickling inside them. And each child's detail revealed not only what the story was about but also something of the child himself.

Facilitating artistic output begins with a good supply of paper which the children feel free to use. A normal eight-and-a-half-by-eleven sheet is too small for the child's coordination at this stage. The larger the sheet of paper, the happier the result is likely to be. Many printing companies offer roll ends of paper at nominal price; butcher paper on the roll will work well.

Wax crayons are the perfect drawing tool for very young children. Give your three-year-old a set of basic colors and encourage him to peel off the paper covers and use all of the different surfaces, not just the pointed end. As the child's coordination improves, he will enjoy drawing with a firm outline. Painting, too, is great fun. Water paint is too pale to be of interest to most children but dry poster paints mixed up make a good, thick paint. Neatest for home use are disks of tempera color or the solid blocks of tempera color that give a firm, bright, poster-paint color when touched with a wet brush. Art educators say that children need a good, thick brush to make the bold, bright outlines they enjoy. Put the water in something as nontippy as you can imagine (such as a sugar bowl) rather than in a tippable glass of water. I found, too, that felt pens served as a good substitute for brush work. In the home, the nontoxic, washable felt pens are easier to have a child work with than are paints. These come inexpensively in packs of as many as twenty-four different shades. All of our children enjoyed the bright, liquid flow of the color that comes from felt pens. Remembering to get the lids back on to prevent the felts from drying was the major problem.

There are many variations on the painting theme. Fingerpainting, if you can stand the mess. Spatter painting with old toothbrushes is great fun—better outdoors than indoors, I have found. Some of the greatest fun my preschoolers had was painting real objects: sleds, wagons, and outbuildings have all been painted. This is messy work, requiring parental help for cleanup. (At least once, such a project resulted in little red footsteps imprinted on my kitchen floor.)

Responding to children's art is very important if they are to continue with it or to enjoy it. One of the important responses, of course, is praise or appreciation: "What a lovely picture." The most common parental mistake in this period of the child's creative development is that of expecting adult realism in their children's art. Many parents say to a child, "That doesn't look like a man. Where's his body? Where are his legs?"

The three- or four-year-old child is not attempting to create realism. He hasn't begun to think, at that point, of making his picture look like a man. He is instead expressing his perception of that reality. Rather than looking for realism, which rarely exists in a young child's drawings, we should be looking for *parallelism*. Cammie-Lou, in her third year, drew pages and pages of big, round, happy faces. Gradually to these were attached various little appendages—two or three fingers sprouting out of the side of the face like whiskers. Later came the toes. Gradually there was the development of the drawing of the total form. To try to hasten this development is to interfere with the child's natural growth in his perceptions of reality. Because of this, many art educators warn against coloring books which impose realism in line on the child's perceptions before he is ready. Coloring books do have some play value, some pastime value, and some coordination value, but they have little or no artistic value.

The joy of children's drawings is that with their drawings they draw you into the world of their perceptions, and you are invited to see as they see. The parent who is interested in helping his child develop creatively does not impose demands upon the child's drawings, does not demand that the child explain omissions, but rather invites the child to tell about his picture. As the child explains what he has drawn, almost always a very interesting rationale becomes apparent to the adult and the door of the childhood mind is thrown ajar.

Your most important response may be in displaying the picture as well as in admiring it. The back of a door, a big bulletin board in a family room, the refrigerator door: these are typical display areas. You do not need to display children's artwork in the living room if you do not wish to, but you will definitely stimulate them to further production if you do display their work where others beside yourself will see and appreciate what they have done.

A little later than the first outburst of drawing will come a stage at which children assemble objects or pieces of fabric and do collage-type work. Some children enjoy cutting and gluing more than others, but almost all can do interesting and expressive work. Mitchell would bring home his Sunday-school papers and items and then carefully cut out various figures and create his own scene by putting these things together again. Heather Ruth has always loved the whole concept of family in a very special way. She has on various occasions gone through old catalogs and magazines and cut out figures that represent our family, juxtaposing them to create a family setting or a family portrait. It was a good opportunity to see how she saw her brothers and sister and her parents. Cammie lavished care on finishing her drawings with glued-on fabric scraps, and Geoffrey liked to cut pictures and words from magazines to create striking posters.

In collage compositions cotton batting can be used for clouds or bunny tails; corrugated cardboard can create the texture for a log house; real cloth can be pasted in place for clothing or curtains. If you keep a bag of scraps available and occasionally suggest that the child might enjoy making a picture with cloth or paper scraps, or cutting pictures out of magazines and putting them together in new ways, you will both stimulate and facilitate this fascinating art form.

This moves us into a whole field of paper-cutting crafts, a good one for finger dexterity as well as artistic expression. For paper projects you will need to keep a pile of old magazines to which the child has access for snipping, and supply blunt-edged scissors. Each of our children had, sometime between age four and six, a big scrapbook into which he was free to paste anything interesting. We called these "Thing Books." Scrapbooks are a way of teaching the child that interesting and lovely things are worthy of being saved and also that memories are something that are worth keeping. A child who likes to save things can have great fun composing albums or scrapbooks. A scrapbook can be a record of a special family trip, of a period of time in the hospital, of the mumps, measles, or chicken pox. My children have helped me assemble their own scrapbooks recording their baby days as well. I had kept the items together in special boxes for each child and when the children were each about six, I gave them a scrapbook and their items and let them assemble their own scrapbook of baby things.

Paper-bag puppets or masks are great fun for preschoolers to make. At kindergarten Heather Ruth one day made a mask, complete with paper curls. She came home and found a small bag from which she constructed an identical mask for her doll. Paper-bag puppets are easy to make. The hand inside the bag activates the "mouth," while the child gives voice to the puppet's personality. Stick puppets made by mounting pictures on sticks are easy to make and move. Old socks with button eyes affixed make fine hand puppets. Marionettes can be made by attaching strings with safety pins to the hands and legs of soft dolls. Tangled strings are a frustrating side effect of this type of puppetry. The joy of simple, homemade puppets is that it allows a craft project to be married to imitative play, and thus creates fascinating play. At the peak of puppet play, our children made puppets and developed story lines for puppet plays. They created a puppet theater from a large box, made and "sold" tickets for their puppet plays, and put on performances.

Preschool children are no longer asked to hem their own hankies or make little undershirts. In the last century, that was expected of them. It suggests that preschoolers are capable of much more refined craft work than we usually think. Needlework is something which children very much enjoy—both boys and girls. It begins with threading cards with shoelace-type thread, and proceeds to various kinds of needle crafts. Children enjoy spool knitting, and the tube of knitting can be curled into various shapes: hot mats for Grandma or Mom, or rugs for the cardboard-box dollhouse floor. Making clothes for their dolls is a favorite kind of needlework for children. The parent's patience and the child's ingenuity are both needed, since coordination is a limiting factor. For preschool children you will be threading needles and counting up to make sure that needles are not lost.

Gift making is a way in which the creative or aesthetic ability of the child can be merged with the pleasure of giving. There are many simple projects that children can make for gifts. One we enjoyed when Geoff and Cammie were tiny was tracing their feet on the backs of old Christmas-card pictures. The children cut the tracing out, and printed on their names and ages to create a bookmark for Grandma or Grandpa's Bible. The ability to make many truly functional items for adults is beyond the child. The child should be encouraged to make something which brings pleasure and which is beautiful in and of itself.

Simpler than gift making and something for which there could be almost endless outlets for the child is the making of cards. For sick or shut-in friends, a child-made card has its own special charm and delight. A child's own handmade cards for special occasions are family treasures. One year I had my children make our Christmas cards. I outfitted them with colorful felt pens and made the folders. The child-designed cards were bright and varied and very "Christmassy."

The basic items which will prompt and aid creativity are not expensive or difficult to have on hand. The parental attitude of tolerance of mess and of encouragement in finding new ways to do things is perhaps the most essential stimulus. When children are involved in craft activities which the mother or the father must continuously, closely supervise, it may well be that the activity is a little too advanced for his stage of development. But parents who do take time out to teach skills, provide materials, and respond with enthusiasm, will help their children discover artistic talents and develop constructive pastimes.

(See the recommended reading list for this chapter at the end of the Source Notes.)

16

Creativity and Language

The child's development in spoken language is a very personal thing.
You can't measure IQ by the date of the onset of intelligible speech.

Jennifer Lise, barely two, visited our home recently. Words
were new and bright as bubbles. Saying many words clearly, she
was also imitating, echoing, repeating words said to her by
others.

When Jenny's mother and I sat down for lunch, Jenny brought
a doll to the table in the doll's high chair. "Baby want bun,"
Jenny announced as we began to eat. Her mother tore off a corner
of a bun and gave it to Jenny to share with her doll. Jenny looked
at it without enthusiasm, then handed it back to her mother.
"Butter on bun," she directed.

"Oh, now," her mother said. "I don't think the baby wants any
butter on her bun. Just a minute. I'll ask her." Turning to the doll,
she asked, "Do you want butter on your bun? No? Okay, then."
Turning back to her little girl, she said, "Baby doesn't want butter, Jenny. She just wants the bun plain."

A few minutes later, we saw Jenny turn to the doll earnestly.
"Baby want butter?" she queried, looking deep into the doll's
bland eyes. "Yes? O-tay, Baby." Her face was just as solemn as
her mother's had been as she handed the piece of bun back to her
mother once again. "Baby want butter on bun now," she said.

For most parents, the development of language ability is one of
the most exciting developments in the life of their preschool child.
Its roots are deep in the tone of loving words whispered to a tiny
baby nursing or being rocked to sleep. Words that soothe and
reassure and firmly tell an infant that someone is in control are
words that build the foundation for good language development.
Many parents don't realize that long before a child can fully un-

derstand the words that are being spoken, he can understand tone and intention. Babies should be talked to—long before they can talk back. There is nothing wrong with talking to a child as though he understands: to your amazement, one day he will show some comprehension. Immersing him in your language will enrich his language development.

And then—very early—at about eight months or younger, a child begins to play with sounds himself. "Mamamamama" usually brings a shout of joy from the mother who has been called by name—despite the fact that it may have been just a fun sound being repeated by the baby who is experimenting with his sound-making equipment of tongue and lips. "Dadadada" may come even earlier. I remember the delight I felt surging through me when my firstborn sat and repeated the sound "abababa."

"He said his first word," I bragged to Cam, "and it was Aramaic!" (And in my heart I had a whole new response to the words, "Ye have received the Spirit of adoption, whereby we cry, Abba, Father" (Romans 8:15 KJV). What a little-child sound "abba" is!)

The child's development in spoken language is a very personal thing. You can't measure IQ by the date of the onset of intelligible speech.

There are a number of specific ways that you can aid your child's all-important language development. Your own clarity of articulation will be important. Never baby talk to your children. It forces them to learn two languages—the "itsy baby coo" that parents use and the normal, garbled English used by the rest of the world. The more clearly you enunciate your words, the more crisply your child is likely to speak. He is likely to reflect your speech patterns with embarrassing accuracy, since as parents you are his prime models for the language which he will use throughout his life. The range of your vocabulary will affect his. There is little need to talk down to children. You may have to explain some difficult words—but generally, children are adept at gleaning meanings from context. The other day, the older children and I were discussing "suicide." Mitchell suddenly spoke up. "That's what that word means," he said with obvious satisfaction. "The other day Cliff said to me, 'Be careful on the swing.

You don't want to commit suicide!' And I didn't know what it was."

Name things for your child. When you go for a little walk, name as many things as you can, clearly and precisely. Instead of saying "birdie" for every bird you see, name the birds. A child can learn that birds have names, somewhat as people do, and can early learn to identify the birds by their names. At a certain point (somewhere around two years), your little one will probably echo every word you say, learning nouns which are the basic building blocks of communication. Later, the same little one will probably drive you crazy by asking, "What's that?" about everything he sees. Give him the answer. Name, name, name. That is how you help your child to gain the building blocks of the language.

You can early begin to play games with sounds.[48] Choose any initial sound and make a string of words beginning with that sound (the way they do on "Sesame Street"). Or build a little story around a basic sound: "Can you come and lick the cream?" Or use some of the old tongue twisters such as, "She sells seashells." Play with words with your preschoolers: it helps them to discover the sheer delight of words which will lead them to enjoy poetry and fine prose as they mature. Reading nursery rhymes is an excellent way to let children play with words. They will gain an ear for sound and a feel for the intrinsic fun of words.

Later on, when the child is between three and four years old, you can begin to play with word meanings, too. Mitchell initiated a "contrariness" word game that he and I played often. He would say, "Get lost," and I would reply, "Get found." "Get young." "Get old." "Get up." "Get down." "Go to sleep." "Wake up." Usually after we ran out of opposites, we would move on to associations. I would say, "Trees," and he would reply, "Branch." I would say, "Hankie," and he would fire back, "Nose." There were no right or wrong answers, only fun associations of opposites or similars to laugh over together.

Another source of language development is your encouragement of children's metaphoric responses. Some children are more metaphoric in their expressions than others, but most will make original and interesting comparisons of one thing to another. "The ducks sit on the pond like a pair of wooden shoes" is a favorite of mine from Cammie-Lou's preschool days. "The jet has strings on it," is another of the children's. A nephew commented, "The moon is like a big balloon bobbing along beside our car."

Your part in encouraging verbal language development is usually just to respond or enter into the games that little discoverers will naturally be playing with their language. Laugh together over words, share fun in making sounds, play with words in as many ways as you and your child can think of. Encourage their approximations and then repeat a difficult word. Correct an incorrect expression without creating a put-down.

But, of course, there is no encouragement to verbal development like the ritual of "Read me a story." It is so important that it cannot be overstressed. In a day of electronic entertainment, a lot of parents do not take time to read to their children, and feel that their children have heard enough stories on TV. But psychologists and reading researchers insist that nothing—but nothing—can replace the warm and happy association with words that comes from the warm relationship of parent, child, and book. Choose a specific story time for your preschoolers. Mine was almost always right after breakfast after Cam had gone out. If I left story time until bedtime, I was running the risk of being too tired to really enjoy the time with the children. But after breakfast we could cozy up together on the couch; each preschooler could choose a book, and we would read together and look at pictures.

The child's verbal development will gradually move from purely oral to visual recognition, and gradually to written language development. How does this happen and how can you help? A mother once asked me for the name of a good workbook to help her four-year-old work with letters. The answer to the question is that there is no such thing. Preschool children should be taught with the widest possible range of incidental learning materials—and need no formal, structured approach such as a workbook. (Admittedly, some five-year-olds get great delight out of "desk work"—especially if they have an older brother or sister in school. That is fine if it is fun, but only so.) Association with books, learning to turn pages sequentially, learning to follow a story from left to right across the page by "reading" pictures: all of this is important "readiness learning" before written language develops.

And when we talk about written language we get into a whole swarm of bees: teachers who don't want parents to teach their children anything; experts who tell the parents that they can teach their children everything at eighteen months. Once again, parents caught in the cross fire often don't know what to do. The answer: Let your child lead you. His interests will be your best pacer. Don't set the goal of teaching your child to read or print, but rather make your goal to stimulate and develop your child's interest in language—and you'll be surprised how much fun you'll have. A reading expert I talked with recently told me that the latest research points out that all kinds of language development at the home level, as long as they are fun and nonpressured, assist in the later development of reading skills.[49] So there is really no way you can hurt the child except, perhaps, by plunking him down and becoming very tense about it being "reading time." As long as language experiences are fun, relaxed, and paced by the child, you can just go along for the ride.

Of course, you can provide some basic stimulation in the form of learning materials: blocks with the alphabet on them are a good start. Sometimes, name the alphabet letters as you pile up the blocks. Then encourage the child to name the letters. Most educators agree that children should learn the capital letters first—but in order to read, they will have to transfer from upper to lowercase letters. I made a game of this with the children. We made one set of cards, each printed with one uppercase letter, and another set of cards with lowercase letters. Then we matched them: "Big *A*—and here's the little *a*." We laughed about how much some of the "babies" or little letters looked like their "mothers"—the uppercase letters.

Other materials for tactile introduction of the alphabet are flocked alphabet cards (I have a beautiful set from Holt, Rinehart & Winston). Try a teaching-materials catalog if you can't find them in a store. Or you can make them by cutting large letters from construction paper or fabric and gluing them on cards. Magnetic letters to play with on the front of the refrigerator while supper is being made are a great idea. Simple words, rhymes, and even little sentences can be put together by pre-schoolers with a little coaching. Have the child start by spelling "at," then see how many words can be made by placing conso-nants in front of the core word: bat, cat, sat, tat, rat, mat, hat.

Learning the names of the alphabet letters is a first step—and it opens up the whole world of literacy. Associating sound with the letters is the next step. "Find me a letter that says 'Ssss.' Now find me a letter that says 'bbbb'," is a delightful game to play with magnetic letters or letter cards. By the way, most commercial flash cards are no good for teaching preschoolers, despite their educational disclaimer. They are too small in print and picture to appeal to preschoolers. You are much better off to build a big set of flash cards on cardboard stock, preferably at least eight and a half by eleven inches, accompanying each letter with a vivid pic-ture cut from a magazine. The process of making such a set of cards with your little ones can be great fun and a good learning experience. I used little mnemonic devices to help my children remember the letter shapes. "*A* looks like a tent, *B* like a fat lady, *H* like goalposts, *S* like a snake."

At the point at which children's interest becomes focused on the written word, making books together is a pleasant activity. A scrapbook, scissors, glue, flow pen, and a stock of old magazines are all that are needed. Have the child choose a picture that interests him and glue it into his book. Then talk about the picture and label it with a clearly printed and correctly spelled word or title. You can have the child think up a little story of several sentences and print that on the facing page. One naming page we had was composed of a toy-company ad, displaying numerous toys. Words such as *car, airplane, barn,* and *house* labeled the toys. At this point the emphasis is not on reading, but on associat-ing written and pictorial symbols.

With this sort of stimulation, it won't be long before your child is taking pencil in hand and doing some writing of his own. He may even learn to read by writing. You can teach him the basic letter shapes as part of his alphabet learning. Most likely he will begin by asking, "How do you make 'dog'?" Sound out the word and print the matching letters on the top of his piece of paper or blackboard. Some of my kids used to follow me around the house with a notebook, writing their words while I worked. And all of my manuscript writing—including this one—has been continuously interrupted by little people asking, "How do you write . . . ?" Associating sound with symbol is the important development at this point, so be sure to sound out the phonic components as you spell.

Perhaps another language tool that you could use is the typewriter. A typewriter is a word machine, and because I have sat many hours at my typewriter, I have been aware of what a great language facilitator it is. I also realized (probably because I read it somewhere) that a typewriter could aid a child in written and verbal expression before his coordination is refined enough for clear printing. I did alphabet play with the two older children by having them sit on my lap and hunt out letters as I described them. "Find that snaky little *S*." "Where's the tall telephone pole called *T*?" Later we wrote little letters to Grandma and Grandpa, using a blend of mnemonics, sound, and just plain pointing to help the little one recognize the letter that came next. Still later, we bought a demonstrator portable typewriter for the ripe sum of twenty-five dollars, so that the children could work on a typewriter without putting my IBM out of adjustment. It has been a boon: all have written stories, created books, and tapped out personal letters on it—more ways of having fun with language.

So the first introduction to the written or coded language may be through the child's own efforts to record primary communication. Have lots of fun with this. Provide a tot with a good, big notebook, a supply of pencils where he can reach them, a clipboard, perhaps, and, if you can, a typewriter. Print letters he asks to see, write out words for him as you sound them, help him to learn to shape the letters. Some children will "take off" with writing skills, sounding out their own funny phonic spellings and creating their own communications. Don't feel that you have to correct the spellings, since this is likely to discourage the child. Enjoy the stories and express your delight—and remember that a good reader is likely to become a good speller, too, all in good time.

By the age of four, the child in an enriched-language environment will have had the following "reading readiness" experiences:

(a) Happy emotional association with books.
(b) Experience in following story sequence through a book.
(c) Experience in left-to-right eye motions.
(d) Knowledge of the alphabet—upper and lowercase letters—not just in rote recitation but in recognition.
(e) Ability to print at least uppercase letters recognizably.
(f) Ability to associate letters with their sounds established through word play and phonic spelling.
(g) Some experiences which establish association of symbol (word) with meaning.

Now you can possibly give him the ultimate key to language development. You can help him "crack the code"—to learn how to read. Learning to read is a complicated and highly individual task. In a school class of thirty, more or less, there is much less chance that the child will learn to crack the code effectively than in a one-to-one relationship with someone who already knows how to read.

Don't push your child to read—just follow his interest in words. Give him a new, easy-to-read book of his very own, or set a first reader aside for him. Talk to him about it. "This is a book you can read for yourself when you want to." Refuse to read that book aloud for your child. It is his to read—when he is ready. When the child shows a keen interest, sit down with him and open the reader. Talk about the pictures and read the title, and then turn the page.

Before letting the child attack the difficult task of reading the words on the page, look at the page as a whole. Talk about the picture. What can the child see there? When he names a key word, show him that word in the printed text and help him see how the letters match the sound—and how the word matches the picture. In this relaxed way, you can help the child learn the two or three key words on the page.

Now invite the child. "Would you like to read this for yourself?" If the child's interest has already been exhausted, let it go at that. Close the book and put it away until another time. By keeping the book out of reach, you will enhance its interest and intrigue for the child. After he has actually begun to read, you will probably leave the book where he can have the pleasure of reading for himself without your help. But at first, putting the book away in a "special reader" place is a good idea. Making reading a special "big boy" or "big girl" activity, something which you obviously place a priority on, will help the child value the activity too.

If the child is ready to begin reading, place your finger under the first word in the text. Ask the child to name the letter and make its sound. Repeat for the next letter. Perhaps your child will already have learned a few little words—this will spare him the pain of sounding out "and" and "but" each time he encounters them, or you can simply supply these "service" words without comment. As the child makes the sounds, you will have to help him blend them into words. You will also have to supply some of the difficult sound blends. Encourage the child to remember words he has already sounded out, to glance back in the text to remind himself of what he has already worked out.

A four-year-old may not want to read more than once a week. A five-year-old may be more persistent in his efforts. In between times, don't push. Remember that the child at home learns at his own pace, consolidating and absorbing each new input before pioneering the next advance in learning. So give your child time. You will find that whether he returns to reading in a week or in a month, he will bring all his previous gains to the task.

It is better to cut the reading time a bit short than to prolong it beyond the child's own interest span and make it unpleasant. Another thing to remember is that a child's sitting span may not be as long as his interest span. When I quit asking my little ones to sit still beside me, and let them wiggle, squirm, kneel down beside the sofa, lie on their backs, and turn the book at any angle that seemed comfortable for the moment, reading sessions were much longer and more relaxed. But remember, the intensive work that is reading requires a kind of concentration that a four- or five-year-old may not be able to muster for more than four or five minutes at a time.

In between reading sessions, you should continue to enjoy the language, to play word and alphabet games, to help the child create his own written expression. Keep the whole process nonlineal: you don't have to do just one tning at a time. And re-member that every nature walk, every trip to the local library, every longer trip your child takes, is enriching his background for reading by giving him an ever-widening range of concepts and contexts to bring to words.

The broader the child's background in the phonic sounds of alphabet letters, creating an orderly predictability to the march of letters across a page, the broader his spoken vocabulary, the broader his association with books, the easier and happier his introduction to reading will be—whether given by you or a teacher at school. And if you do teach your child to read before he goes to school, be prepared for some disappointments.

His teacher may be less than delighted. Not every teacher has the flexibility to know how to challenge the student who does not "fit." Or, as one of my children did, your reader may simply stop reading when he goes to school. Geoff discovered that the other children in Grade One were not reading yet, and decided to con-form. But I found that once his social adjustments were made, he was able to resume his reading without loss of skill. So, even though first-grade adjustments may be somewhat complicated, I still feel that the child who is given language enrichment and even preliminary reading training at home has the best possible start in the exciting process of unlocking knowledge from books.

Because language is so individual, each child will approach learning to read as individually as he approaches all other kinds of learning. The observant and sensitive parent is probably best equipped to know what combination of activities will work best for a particular child. But whether or not parents decide to actu-ally teach a preschooler to read is relatively incidental. Any home that provides a child with a rich background of pleasurable as-sociation with language, with an early alertness to sounds, with a broad range of personal experiences, and a foundation of love for books, will prepare children for a lifetime of effective reading.

"In the beginning was the Word" (John 1:1 KJV). Christians have shared the Judaic heritage as "people of the Book," with a unique interest in the sanctity and power of words. Christian parents today can maintain that tradition by helping our children into the world of words within our homes.

17

Kids and Good Books

By what criteria shall we determine which books are good?

"Dad sometimes wore cardboard in his shoes," writer Charles Paul Conn reminisces, "but he always seemed to have a dollar or two for books. Each child got a dime for reading and reporting to Dad on a book. For something off the classic shelf such as *Pilgrim's Progress,* he'd pay a bonus. We'd save the money and go buy more books." [50] The heritage of books is one we should share generously. Our children have teethed on books, sat on books, and, at an early age, read books. I'd like to share with you some of the books we have found helpful, and some of the approaches to books that parents can use to help their children into the world of good books.

We are experiencing a publication explosion. This means that there is a wider selection of children's literature now available on the market than at any prior time. The result is that good books are available for our children at reasonable cost, but they are competing on the marketplace with much mediocre material. We want our children to have access not only to books but to *good* books as well. By what criteria, then, shall we determine which books are good? The very best books are books which combine several of the values listed below. But many good books will be good because of their contribution to the child in one of the value areas.

1. Aesthetic value. A beautiful book is one which is attractive because of its form, its art content, or because of its balance of beautiful art and graceful language. The most obvious attraction to children will be visual. Watch the delight with which children greet a book illustrated by Brian Wildsmith. Preschoolers love color, yet they are equally fascinated by pen-and-ink drawings such as the famous Shepherd drawings for *Winnie the Pooh*. Good books should introduce children to a wide range of beauty: from fine pencil sketches such as those by Dorothy Lathrop through to the richly simple art of Eliza Jack Keats, with collage textures that are almost palpable.

2. Interest value. A good book is an interesting book. It may be interesting because it is teaching the child something new, as with the fine *National Geographic* publications for children, or because the experiences parallel those of the child. *Let's Be Enemies* and *I Hate Dogs* are of this type. A book may be interesting because of its detail. In this field the Richard Scarry books lead the day.

3. Humor value. A book may be good because it is funny. Most funny books have other kinds of significance as well, but of course there are books such as the Dr. Seuss "Bright and Early"—designed simply to introduce children to the world of words in a way that is fun. Laughing together over a funny book is one of the joys of the parent who spends time with his little ones.

4. Truth value. When we come to Christian books, we need to bring these same criteria. To think that a book is a good book just because it contains a "good message" is really to underestimate our children's needs and their ability to appreciate aesthetic values, interest values, and humor values. The best books in the Christian field for children will combine at least some of these values with the message of the Bible, or with the message of the reality of Jesus Christ in the individual's life. For parents who would like to investigate further ways in which to judge books, I recommend Gladys Hunt's excellent little handbook *Honey for a Child's Heart* (Zondervan, 1969). It should be a standard reference work for Christian parents, with its excellent text and bibliography.

The single clearest thing that should emerge from any review of children's literature is that if you are going to invite your children into the world of good books, you will give them a wide variety of books. Some you will choose because they are funny. Some will be bought because they are easy to read. Some we will make available because they have a beautiful story to which the child can respond.

The ultimate criterion of whatever books or reading material we bring into our home should be that of Philippians 4:8 NAS: "Whatever is true, whatever is honorable, whatever is right, whatever is pure, whatever is lovely, whatever is of good repute, if there is any excellence and if anything worthy of praise, let your mind dwell on these things." [51]

For the youngest child, the ideal book is one with very large illustrations and a few words. For the book which he is going to be allowed to handle and manipulate himself, the plasticized books such as the C. R. Gibson "Little Plastic Books," or washable cloth books are ideal. These books are virtually indestructible. We have one which survived the teething years of all four children, somewhat chewed and dog-eared, but still intact. Children should learn to hold books, to feel books, to turn pages, just as early as they show any interest. These tough little books can take it.

From the book which is designed mostly to introduce the child to the act of turning pages, we move toward books which combine artwork and story—the "Read to me" storybooks of which there are now many on the market. The Concordia Arch Book series led the way in bringing a whole new look to the Bible-story idea—giving the children vivid contemporary illustrations, catchy rhymes, and occasionally very beautiful prose-poetry as in *The Little Sleeping Beauty* and *The Little Boat That Almost Sank*.

Another entry in the field of contemporizing the Bible storybook is the Muffin Family series by V. Gilbert Beers (Moody Press). This series couples Bible stories with contemporary application stories. An outstanding feature of these books is the art: beautiful and delightful and funny.

We have always made use of library resources as well as buying books. We have in our home the World Book Childcraft series with its rich resources of stories and poetry, as well as Marguerite DeAngeli's *Book of Nursery and Mother Goose Rhymes* (Doubleday), which is the delight of bouncing English rhymes and lovely pencil sketches. A set of books which are neither beautiful to look at nor great literature but which still command the loyalty of children are the Thornton Burgess Bedtime Stories. The children enjoy the humor and pathos of the talking animals.

My own personal delight in Winnie the Pooh has been translated into several readings with the children. The special joy of *Winnie the Pooh* and *The House at Pooh Corner* is that you read them once and chuckle; read them the second time and laugh; and by the third or fourth time you laugh in anticipation of the humor. Mitchell and I in particular have laughed together over Winnie the Pooh. And A. A. Milne's little rhymes, *When We Were Very Young* and *Now We Are Six,* vie with Robert Louis Stevenson's *A Child's Garden of Verses* for first place in children's poetry.

In the wide field of children's periodicals, two are worth the attention of Christian parents. The *National Geographic* children's magazine *World* is full of beautiful photography and fascinating nature lore. For literature and art, *Cricket* stands out above all similar magazines.

Very early reading materials need to be carefully selected. The story needs to be simply told, of course. But extreme limitation of vocabulary may not be as important as intrinsic interest or funniness in the story. *Go, Dog, Go* in the Dr. Seuss reading series ("Bright and Early Books for Beginning Beginners") is excellent. So is Else Holmelund Minarik's near-perfect *Little Bear* (in the Harper and Row "I CAN READ" series). Perhaps one of the biggest deterrents to reading is that many primer stories are not worth the intense effort reading requires of a little child.

When actually teaching your child to read, find out what reader series your school uses and scrupulously avoid using that. You are probably safe with Christian-reader series (unless, of course, your children will be attending a Christian day school). Our children learned to read through *Basic Bible Readers* (Standard Publishing). We now also have a set of the new *Learning to Read From the Bible Series* by V. Gilbert Beers (Zondervan). Because they were learning to read about the Lord Jesus or learning to read Bible stories, our children were excited with what they were reading. The effort that sometimes brought perspiration to their foreheads seemed to them worthwhile.

As our children reached a basic proficiency level in their readers, we gave them their first Bibles. We chose from the *Lol-*

lipop Series (Zondervan) for our children's first Bibles. The King
James Version was still used most generally in our church and it
seemed important to us to have the children have a Bible that
would coincide with what the minister was reading from. Each
child chose his own color, and so we have a green Bible, a brown
Bible, a black Bible, and a blue one—reminders of milestones in
reading for each child. Since then, the children have also been
given copies of some other translations.

There are many lovely children's Bibles available today. I like
the children's edition of the New International Version. This edition features large type and key verses set out in clear print in the
"memory margin"—an open invitation to memory work. Now
both the Old and New Testaments are available in this version.
The children's edition of the Living Bible is less attractive, despite some lovely Richard and Francis Hook illustrations. The
very small print is difficult for children's eyes to follow. The Bible
Society's Good News Bible (Today's English Version) has imaginative and fluid line drawings—several on every page. It is
probably the best-illustrated Bible available.

In choosing a Bible for a child, you must first determine which
translation you wish. You should take into consideration what
translation is in most common usage in your church. You should
also choose a translation suitable to family Bible reading. We are
in the somewhat confusing situation of being a transition generation as far as Bible translation is concerned. By the next generation there will, I hope, be more general consensus. Perhaps by
that time either the New American Standard or the New International Version will have gained the hearts of a large enough sector
of Christian public that there will be more standardization.
Meanwhile, we must evaluate translations carefully and make
our personal choice.

Having decided upon translation, I would give attention to additional features: size of print, size of illustrations, and explana-
tory notes could be considered. Children do not need cross-
references, India-thin paper, or expensive leather covers in order
to have the thrill of "a Bible of my own."

Children move from early reading experiences to reading the
Word of God themselves: a natural and rewarding progression in

the Christian home. Then, with a sure base in the Word of God, our children can reach out to all the world of good books and great authors: from Beverly Cleary and Carolyn Haywood to Laura Ingalls Wilder and Louisa May Alcott; from A. A. Milne to C. S. Lewis, Madeleine de l'Engle, and Tolkien. The golden chain will lead on and on. We will encourage them to read, read, read, evaluating all by the plumb line of Scripture. And we will encourage them to respond to good books with gratitude to God, the Giver of everything, everywhere, that is truly good.

18

Creative Thinking

If we want our children to realize their creative potential for God, we need to help them become not only competent, confident, and creative children, but also reflective, analytical, thinking children.

I was in grade two—and beginning to join in with the others in the after-dinner family Bible reading. Eager to show off my reading ability, I had made an agreement with my mother. "I want to read all by myself," I told her. "Don't help me anymore unless I'm really stuck."

I chugged through a verse in Psalms, sounding out the difficult words; then, flushed with my victory, I came to an abrupt halt. The last word of the verse looked like no word I had ever seen before. I attempted sounding. The sounds made no connection with reality for me. Finally, I looked across the kitchen nook to my mother.

"Stop and think," my mother said softly.

"But I have," I wailed. "And I still can't get it!"

Then my mother laughed. "Oh, it's the *word* you need help with! I thought you wanted the meaning." And so I came to know the little word *selah,* the musical notation in the Psalms which indicated a pause, or, as my mother had simplified it for me, a time to "stop and think."

I don't know why that little incident has stayed so clearly in my mind, but I share it because I think there need to be some *selahs*—some times to just "stop and think" in our children's lives. If we want our children to realize their potential for God, we need to help them become not only competent, confident, and creative children but also reflective, analytical, thinking children. Jesus in the Temple at age twelve, both hearing and asking questions (Luke 2:46), represents best this quality we desire to develop in our children.

1. Acquisition of knowledge. All thinking must begin with the acquisition of knowledge.[52] Children have two basic facilities which enhance their ability to acquire knowledge. The first is their curiosity, and the second is their ability to memorize and retain facts once acquired. The adult in the home becomes a central learning resource, fielding questions as they occur. Several years ago when I had little questioners around me all the time, I wrote this little couplet in my notebook:

> A little voice is talking, asking
> questions one a minute.
> Give me Lord, your grace, to give
> each answer with truth in it.

Taking children's questions seriously and answering courteously and completely is perhaps the most important way in which parents can help their children to become thinking persons. The seriousness with which curiosity is met places a value on questioning—and questions are the doors by which we all open our minds to knowledge and understanding.

There are at least three ways in which a thinking parent can lead a child beyond his own question asking to more complex thought processes. One is to greet the child's interest with enthusiasm and lead him beyond merely gaining an answer—and thus restoring equilibrium to his mind—to asking additional questions on the topic. The child who asks, "Do all bees sting?" should be given more than the obvious answer of no. The learning dialogue might go this way:

Child (age four): Do all bees sting?
Parent: No. Some bees are equipped to sting and some are not.
Child: How can you tell the difference?
Parent: Probably it is smartest to act as if they can all sting just now—but we can look it up in our book about bees.

Child and parent look up the article on bees in an encyclopedia or other resource book. A younger child may want only to look at a picture. An older child may wish to have the article read to him. If the parent is too busy to follow up the child's interest at that moment, the topic could be left open as follows:

> Parent: I'm sure we could find out a lot of interesting things about bees. Tomorrow at story time, we'll look up what we can find out about them.

Such a promise should probably be noted on a calendar so that it can be carried through at a later time.

By the time a child is five, the parent should have demonstrated the use of reference books in the house or library enough to be able to say, "Go find the encyclopedia that has *B* on the back of it and look for the article on bees. See what you can find out for yourself. I'll read what you find."

With just this kind of dialogue and "leading on," one of our preschoolers made a personal study of hummingbirds; another one had a passion for dinosaurs. There have been dozens of other "research projects," individual quests for knowledge, which have grown out of children's questions and my nudging them to find out more.

The second way in which parents can help their children think through and beyond questions is to refuse to answer some questions. Now that may appear to contradict the basic principle of question answering. But when children ask questions to which the answer is obvious, or to which the child could, himself, discover the answer by deduction, then the parent should lead the child to answer his own question by putting the evidence together to form the whole.

Third, the parent can help the child to think by asking questions of the child. The parent who asks his child to explain things to him (beyond just the unanswerable "Why did you spill your milk?") helps the child to think inductively and deductively.

While a child will acquire knowledge primarily through question asking, he can also be encouraged to become an accurate and patient observer. This is one of the results of a questioning parent. Looking at a footprint in the sandy road behind our home, I ask Mitchell: "Which way was the deer going? How do you know? Was it alone? Was the other deer a little one or a big one? How do you know?'' Children are naturally observant, but they can have their abilities to perceive heightened by parents who take delight in detail, who point out things to the child, and who respond enthusiastically when a child reports the results of his observations. A bird book covering the birds of your area, and books giving the names of the vegetation found in your region, are worthwhile investments. Help your child identify birds and wild flowers by looking them up and you will help your children develop not only in knowledge but also in precision of observation.

One of the most exciting things about watching children acquire knowledge is seeing how quickly and how accurately they are able to remember. Children's memories serve to provide, between the age of birth and six years, a phenomenal fund of recoverable information on which the child can build his later learning.[53] Because little children memorize easily, because they "trap" facts and information so effectively, teaching them is the most rewarding of all teaching experiences. While rote memorizing has fallen out of favor in educational method, almost all of us treasure bits and pieces of poetry and Scripture learned while we were very young. There is nothing wrong with utilizing the memorizing capabilities of little children to provide them with a stock of ideas, of poetry, of Scripture verses. When helping children to actually memorize, the parents should remember to keep it a game, making it fun. Unpleasant learning experiences will probably be transferred as an unpleasant association with the material that is learned. Extrinsic rewards, best related to the material that is learned (an *Arch Book* for learning the Beatitudes, for example), can provide motivation for the learning process.

2. Application and projection. Beyond merely acquiring knowledge, children can be helped to think about logical outcomes. Piaget has brought to our attention that children's grasp of causation is at best tenuous throughout most of the preschool phase. However, parents who point out cause and effect can help the child become aware of predictable trends. These can be as simple as noticing that night follows day or spring follows winter. Or they can be as complex as noting that disobedience produces unhappiness and obedience produces happiness. Helping children predict the outcomes of their actions—a carelessly stacked pile of books will soon come sliding down; a milk glass placed at the edge of the table will probably result in a spill—helps children become aware of logical connections between cause and effect. Another kind of "going beyond" is to read the children part of a story and have them construct an ending.

Application is using acquired or "known" knowledge and applying it to a real-life situation or problem. It can be as simple as the following:

Child: What day is it today?
Parent: What day was yesterday?
Child: Saturday.
Parent: Then what day is today?
Child: Sunday. Are we going to church?
Parent: What do we always do on Sunday morning?
Child: Go to church. What shall I wear?
Parent: What clothes do we usually wear to church?
Child: Our Sunday clothes. I'll wear my suit.

3. Synthesis. The next level of critical thinking is synthesis, the creating of a new communciation or product using the knowledge acquired and the application and projection skills learned. A type of synthesis would be to plan a day or a morning's activities. Quite often my five-year-old comes to me with a pencil and says, "Let's plan my day," and he and I discuss what he would like to get accomplished. Then we print out a little list for him.

Another kind of creative synthetic thinking is brainstorming for solutions to a problem. The rules for brainstorming are quite simple, and often allow for productive creative thought.

(a) The problem is stated: "I have a meeting this afternoon which won't be interesting to you. What shall we plan for you?"

(b) Ideas are invited and noted *without judgment:*

"I could stay alone."
"Could Grandma come over and play?"
"I could go to Kristi's house."
"I could bring a book and come to the meeting with you."

(c) After all alternatives have been offered, each is explored as to feasibility. The preschooler can't be left at home alone, and Grandma is sick with a cold—so parent and child can make a decision between the other alternatives.

(d) A decision is reached. When a child has made inputs and assisted in the evaluation, the final decision just might be mutually agreeable to parent and child!

Yet another kind of synthesis is creating metaphor. Almost as soon as the child can speak, he creates metaphors. It is one of the ways in which a limited vocabulary can handle an ever-increasing number of objects and concepts. I recall a three-year-old in our house saying, "I love you, Mom, like pickles and chocolate bars and ice cream." That's not such a long step away from "O, my Luve is like a red, red rose . . ." after all. Metaphoric thought patterns enrich observation and open the way to the enjoyment of literature. Writing or telling stories; producing puppet plays; writing personal letters—all of these involve synthesis in bringing elements together to form a new whole. So, too, do the various creative crafts we have already discussed.

4. Critical evaluation. Finally, we want to have our children emerge as evaluative and critical thinkers. When a child reads a book or has a book read to him, there is nothing wrong with asking, "Did you like that book?" Most children will respond at first with a yes or a no. Later, you may proceed with a more probing, "Why did you like that book? What do you like about that book? Why do you pick this book more often than your other ones?" Asking the child to evaluate can help him to begin to discriminate between good books and better. It is well, however, to remember that most of children's judgments are intuitive. If a child does not respond to verbalizing reasons for his preferences, do not frustrate him by pressing for this.

We are in need of discerning Christians. We need for our own selves and for our children the development of criteria by which products, television programs, books, and actions can be judged. Basic moral criteria will be based upon the Word of God. In addition, we can learn aesthetic criteria, and criteria which have to do with the integrity of a piece of work. I believe that we are experiencing a dearth of discernment because we have been brainwashed to think that discerning is the opposite of love; that somehow we should be awash in a sea of love without any critical facilities. Paul prayed for the Philippian church, "That your love may abound yet more and more in knowledge and in all judgment; That ye may approve things that are excellent" (Philippians 1:9, 10 KJV).

Whether it is dish drying or bed making; whether it is a letter written or a garden row hoed: the goal held out to our children and the criteria by which they should be discerningly judged and judging, is that of excellence—not, please note, of perfection. We discourage our children and defraud ourselves of the fruit of human effort if we ask for perfection. Perfection is an attribute of God. It is beyond man's reach. But excellence: that top-notch performance in whatever we do is a goal well worth setting for our children, well worth pursuing for ourselves, and well worth demanding in the material we are looking at today.

The evangelical Christian world has produced a body of writing, of cinema, and of music, which has tended tragically toward the mediocre, and this needs to be remedied. If our Gospel is hidden, it will surely be hidden to those who are lost but who have higher literary and aesthetic criteria than we have ourselves. We must teach our children to dare to discern.

Of course the corollary danger to the virtue of discernment is the vice of arrogance or harshness. We need to teach our children early that we may judge a book as a work of art; we may judge words as to their aptness; we may judge an action as to its morality or its appropriateness. But we have no right to judge the person. The person producing the work or the word or the action stands before God and before God alone. And we are all on a par with any person—all sinners in the eyes of God with only one claim to redemption, the sacrifice of Jesus Christ. And so discernment must constantly and consciously be tempered by humility.

The advantages of the home as a laboratory in which thinking can be stimulated are profound. In almost any other learning environment a child is locked into a line of learning situations in which reading is done at ten o'clock and spelling at eleven o'clock—completely independent of the child's particular interests at the moment. But in the home, a mother and father can respond to their child's interests at that moment. Thus, four or five minutes of home teaching may be equivalent to an hour of school teaching when a subject of limited interest to the child is introduced at a time of limited interest in the child. In an enriched home environment, many kinds of learning processes happen simultaneously, and much is learned by osmosis. Children simply absorb knowledge, values, criteria, and attitudes. Furthermore, in the home, the learning and thinking process is not separated from the valuing process as it is so often in the school.

Creative children must be critical children—in the best possible sense of the word: "Exercising or involving careful judgment."[54] While recognizing that children's full cognitive powers will not be reached during the preschool phase, we can diligently lay a foundation for the exercise of careful judgment in all areas of life. A balanced approach has respect both to logic and intuition; both to analysis and synthesis.

Thinking children are children whose questions are answered, and children who learn to answer questions in turn. They are children who are alert and observant, and who are constantly encouraged to create new structures—in words, in crafts, in play. Ultimately, it is our prayer that thinking children will be able to choose between the better and the best throughout their lives.

19

Getting It Together

Recognizing that children thrive best in an atmosphere of regularity and order, we will attempt to develop some recognizable rhythms of life.

There's a page in one of my old coil notebooks that I especially like. Across the top of it are my handwritten words, " 'God is not the author of confusion, but of order.' I must get better organized." The rest of the page is filled in with the whirling scribbles typical of a two-year-old. Somehow, just after having penned that admirable resolution, I had been called away—and one of my toddlers completed the page for me. It is a perfect vignette of living with little ones: trying to create order amidst the continuous demands and disruptions which threaten total chaos.

How can parents with several preschoolers organize time and priorities to reflect the threefold emphasis of confidence, character, and creativity? Schedules just don't work. Dental appointments, shopping trips, Aunt Mary's two-week visits: all of these interrupt the timetable. So do teething, toilet training, measles, and mumps. But if we know our broad basic goals clearly enough, we won't have to timetable in order to accomplish them. We can move toward them, day by day, "here a little, there a little," all the time.

Recognizing that children thrive best in an atmosphere of regularity and order, we will attempt to develop some recognizable rhythms of life. Fixed mealtimes, story times, and bedtimes can form a structure within which family living moves fluidly. What we need to develop in a home with little children is *flexible order*. Horatius Bonar makes this classic statement concerning time management:

> There needs not be routine, but there must be regularity; there ought
> not to be mechanical stiffness, but there must be order . . . .[55]

What I like most about that statement is that, unlike many wise
things said by men, it actually is workable in the home situation
with preschoolers.

Within the basic structures, there needs to be broad flexibility.
There must be lots of time for unplanned, spontaneous activity.
There must be time taken for questions, and time for dealing with
tears. There must be, at least once in a while, time to stop and just
let the clock tick unnoticed as parents enjoy the comradeship and
companionship of little children. And sometimes, time must be
taken to "make a memory"—to do something special and
memorable.

Tranquility on the part of the parent in charge is perhaps the
most important key to peace and order in the home—and that is
not always easy to achieve. Nerve endings seem to fray out with
the continuous demands of nurturing little ones. I recall that,
after my third baby was born, there seemed to be no cessation in
those demands. By the time I had fed and bathed the baby,
another little one needed my time and attention, and then
another. Exhausted and tense after childbirth, I sang a little
chorus, "Let there be peace on earth, and let it begin with me,"
again and again.[56] And what I meant as I hummed was, "Let
there be peace in this home; let there be peace in this family; and
let it start here, with me."

As I floundered through winter days with two toddlers and one
infant, I reminded myself "to take each moment and live each
moment in peace, eternally." I prayed for peace so that I could
really feel the baby's soft skin. To pause and let her fingers curl
around mine. To coax the sudden smile as I changed her. And, at
the same time, to really enjoy the two-year-old who was so eager
to help. "Now can I pepper the baby?" she would ask, mistaking
the baby powder for the similar shaker on the table. And to answer the thousand and one questions of an eager four-year-old,
too. Day after day, I hummed that song and prayed, consciously
preparing myself spiritually for the incredible demands of each
child. "And the peace of God, which surpasses all comprehen-

sion,'' guarded my heart and mind in Christ Jesus. (Philippians 4:7 NAS).

Perhaps one of the most important secrets I learned in those at-home years was that I, too, had needs. I found it much easier to meet the pressing needs of my family if some of my own personal needs were also being met.

Recently I had a phone call from a lovely young mother with three very young children. She was tired and discouraged. ''I work all day just to keep up. And when I'm finished, I just have to start all over.''

''Tell me something,'' I said. ''What do you like to do best?''

''What do you mean?'' she asked, baffled.

''I mean, what activity would be a treat for *you?*''

''That's easy,'' Anna said. ''I love to sew. But,'' she added wistfully, ''I never have time anymore.''

''Okay,'' I said. ''Now tell me—what's the quietest hour of the day—the time when one or two are napping and the pace slows down a bit?''

She thought for a minute. ''Well—usually there's a little while right after lunch.''

''Listen: grab that hour for yourself.''

She gasped, ''But I'm already behind!''

''I know,'' I said. ''But if you are going to enjoy those children and your husband, and not turn into a martyr, you have to have something to look forward to *for yourself.* Organize around the sewing. Push your work ahead in the morning, work like crazy later in the afternoon, and take that hour, right after lunch, to do your sewing.''

She tried it. When she phoned back a few weeks later, she was exuberant. ''It's great,'' she said. ''I'm getting to sew—and my work's not any further behind. You know something? I'm even *feeling* better!''

I had shared with Anna what I had found worked for me. When I took an hour a day for reading and writing, the days were brighter, shorter, tighter. I disciplined myself both to ''do my thing,'' and to keep it in balance with the needs of my family. The delightful spin-off of this procedure is that the parent who is engaged in creative activity herself is also patterning or modeling creative activities for her children. Gordon Cosby, pastor of the celebrated Church of the Saviour in Washington, D.C., says, "The most effective thing we can do to call forth the gift of another is to employ our own gift in freedom." [57]

If we are to call forth the creative gifts within our little children, we need to be actively creative in our own lives. By making time for the fulfilling of our own needs, we find, too, that we have more energy, more health, more vigor and joy in serving our families.

In recognizing that we do have needs, we recognize that we are failure-prone and imperfect creatures. Mother doesn't always know best—and neither does Father. We make mistakes—proofs of our humanity, I guess. And we must early recognize that our children will not be perfect, any more than we are. They will have some hang-ups. They will grow up and look back over their shoulders and say, "If my parents had just . . ." or "If only they hadn't." Hopefully, they will determine to improve upon our parenting with their own children.

Because of our own weaknesses and inabilities, we are humbly dependent upon God our Father for wisdom and strength. We will trust, simply, that by the grace of God our children will grow up equipped for God's service.

We will trust that through us and in spite of us, "All [our] children shall be taught of the Lord; and great shall be the peace of [our] children" (Isaiah 54:13 KJV). In our children's lives, the foundation for all true confidence, all real character, all meaningful creativity will be salvation through faith in Jesus Christ (1 Corinthians 3:11). Upon this foundation, the twin pillars of confidence and character can support a lifetime of creative service. Without this foundation, the whole structure will collapse into the shifting sands of fallen human nature. [58]

Parents are a badly put-down group these days. They are weighted with huge responsibility, while warnings are issued on all sides. They are full of fear about damaging psyches, limiting creativity, and producing "not OK" feelings in their children. As Christian parents we need to affirm our vocation to parenthood as a sacred calling. Our task is carried out under Him and by His grace. Only so can we produce children who can demonstrate and articulate the Christian message for yet another generation, children with the confidence and the character to be creative in the service of their Lord and Saviour, Jesus Christ.

> May the God of peace make you perfect and holy; and may you all be kept safe and blameless, spirit, soul and body, for the coming of our Lord Jesus Christ. *God has called you and he will not fail you.*
>   1 Thessalonians 5:23, 24 JERUSALEM BIBLE (*italics added*)

SOURCE NOTES

Chapter 2 **Confident Parents/Confident Kids**

1. James Dobson, *Hide or Seek* (Old Tappan, New Jersey: Fleming H. Revell, 1974), pp. 9–14.
2. The warning re: "overparenting" was made by Betty Friedan in *The Feminine Mystique* (New York: W. W. Norton, 1963), pp. 183–189 and chapter 12, "Progressive Dehumanization," p. 263.

   Gail Sheehy comments in *Passages* (New York: Bantam, 1977), p. 56:

   > Parents can offer lessons and clubs and family trips . . . but in the giving somewhat contaminate almost anything they give because it is an extension of their rules and values.

   Thomas Gordon, author of *Parent Effectiveness Training* (New American Library, 1975), states in chapter 10, "Parental Power: Necessary and Justified?":

   > The stubborn persistence of the idea that parents must and should use authority in dealing with children has, in my opinion, prevented for centuries any significant change or improvement in the way children are raised . . . . All parents talk easily about authority, but few can define it or even identify the source of their authority (p. 164).

3. *Compare* Ephesians 6:1–4 and 1 Timothy 3:2–5 with a positive example of parenting in the Old Testament (Genesis 18:19) and a negative example (1 Samuel 3:11–13). In both doctrine and example, the principle of authority exercised over children, with direct responsibility and answerability to God for the way in which it is exercised, is very clear.
4. Watchman Nee, *The Normal Christian Life* (Fort Washington: Christian Literature Crusade, 1958).
5. God knows individuals from conception: Genesis 25:23; Psalm 139. God knows people by name: Genesis 17:5; 32:28; Psalms 91:14. God is concerned about the development of individuals: Galatians 1:15–19; *compare* Acts 9:15, 16. God orders our circumstances to bring about His purposes: Romans 8:28–30. Example: Joseph, *see* Genesis 37–50; *note especially* Genesis 50:20.

6. This phrase is one I gleaned from a seminar on "Communicating Our Faith," given by Marj Long, Inter-Varsity Christian Fellowship staff member, University of Alberta campus.

Chapter 4 **Confidence and Self-Acceptance**

7. Erik H. Erikson, *Identity: Youth and Crisis* (New York: W. W. Norton, 1968), p. 91.
8. _____, *Insight and Responsibility* (New York: W. W. Norton, 1964), p. 116.
9. John Calvin, *Institutes of the Christian Religion,* 111:3 (Grand Rapids: Wm. B. Eerdmans, 1975), p. 52.
10. The value of individual differences is pointed out by Paul in a number of passages on gifts of the Spirit: Ephesians 4; 1 Corinthians 12; Romans 12.
11. Thomas A. Harris, *I'm OK–You're OK* (New York: Avon Books, 1967), pp. 47–59.
12. Burton L. White, *The First Three Years of Life* (Englewood Cliffs: Prentice-Hall, 1975), p. 142. This book is a most useful handbook for parents of very young children, detailing developmental sequences from birth to the third birthday.
13. In Genesis 5:29, there is a most interesting "window" into the remote past when children were welcomed as fellow workers.

Chapter 5 **Confidence and Reassurance**

14. William Golding, *Lord of the Flies* (London: Faber and Faber, 1954). In this novel, a small boy's dream of a "snake-thing" or "beastie" both embodies and foreshadows the manifestation of evil in the nature of the shipwrecked boys (p. 39).
15. Bruno Bettelheim, *The Uses of Enchantment* (New York: Alfred A. Knopf, 1976). A very interesting and illuminating study of the value of fairy tales in children's development.

Chapter 6 **Confidence and Competence**

16. Erikson, *Identity,* pp. 107–114.
17. Ibid., p. 123

Chapter 7 **The Ultimate Confidence**

18. Bettelheim, *Enchantment,* p. 7.
19. Andrew Murray, *How to Raise Your Children for Christ* (Minneapolis: Bethany Fellowship, 1975), p. 172
20. Roy B. Zuck and Gene A. Getz, *Christian Youth: An In-Depth Study* (Chicago: Moody Press, 1968), p. 41.

Chapter 8 **Not Just Confidence—Character**

21. Murray, *Raise Your Children,* p. 11.
22. John McDermott, ed., *The Writings of William James* (New York: The Modern Library, 1967), p. 20.

Chapter 9 **Discipline for Self-Discipline**

23. *Webster's New Collegiate Dictionary* (Springfield: G. & C. Merriam Company, 1960), "discipline."
24. Sheehy, *Passages,* p. 49.
25. This distinction is made by Francis A. Schaeffer in *The God Who Is There* (Downer's Grove: Inter-Varsity Press, 1968), pp. 102, 106.
26. White, *First Three Years,* pp. 140, 141.
27. David Riesman, *The Lonely Crowd* (New Haven: Yale University Press, 1950), pp. 16, 24. Riesman sees "inner direction" as typical of the aims and outcomes of child rearing in a "society that emerged with the Renaissance and Reformation and that is only now vanishing . . ." (p. 14). In today's society, he sees "other-directedness" as the mode, producing people whose "contemporaries are the source of direction . . . . The goals toward which the other-directed person strives shift with that guidance" (p. 21). I am arguing that Christian parents will opt for child-rearing practices that are conducive to inner-directedness, despite these changes in our society at large.

Chapter 10 **A Firm Foundation**

28. Roy B. Zuck and Robert E. Clark, *Childhood Education in the Church* (Chicago: Moody Press, 1975), p. 18.
29. Elisabeth D. Dodds, *Marriage to a Difficult Man* (Philadelphia: Westminster Press, 1971), p. 48.
30. Chaim Potok, *In the Beginning* (Greenwich: Fawcett Books, 1976), p. 383.
31. C. S. Lewis, *Letters to Malcolm: Chiefly on Prayer* (London: Geoffrey Bles, 1964), p. 118.

Chapter 11 **Handling the Great Competitor**

32. Nathan Isaacs, *A Brief Introduction to Piaget* (New York: Schocken Books, 1975), p. 18.
33. Parenthetical paraphrases are from The Living Bible, Copyright © 1971 by Tyndale House Publishers, Wheaton, Illinois 60187.
34. Dr. Robert Lieber, quoted on Canadian Broadcasting Corporation evening news, "The National," February 10, 1976.
35. Dr. Robert Lieber, quoted in "Violence on TV May Affect Sanity," *Edmonton Journal,* Wednesday, February 11, 1976.

36. Richard Goranson, *Television Violence Effect: Issues and Evidence,* report of Ontario Royal Commission on Violence, quoted in *Financial Post,* March 12, 1977.
37. Quoted from interview on "As It Happens," CBC, April 6, 1976.
38. Marie Winn, *The Plug-In Drug* (New York: Viking, 1977), as quoted in the *Edmonton Journal,* Saturday, February 26, 1977.
39. Louis Sabin, article in *Today's Health,* February, 1972, p. 71.
40. Zuck and Getz, *Christian Youth,* pp. 45, 48, 49, 59, 158.

Chapter 12   **Body Truth**

41. E. Margaret Clarkson, *Susie's Babies* (Grand Rapids: Wm. B. Eerdmans, 1960).
42. Marguerite Kurth Frey, *I Wonder, I Wonder* (St. Louis: Concordia Publishing House, 1967).
43. *About Me.* 1968 Childcraft Annual (Chicago: Field Enterprises Educational Corporation).
44. Erwin Kolb, *Parents' Guide to Christian Conversation About Sex* (St. Louis: Concordia Publishing House, 1967).
45. Dr. Haim G. Ginott, *Between Parent and Child* (New York: Macmillan, 1965). Chapter 9 "Sex Education" is very helpful.

Chapter 13   **Creativity Begins at Home**

46. Erik H. Erikson, *Childhood and Society* (New York: W. W. Norton, 1950), pp. 237, 238.
47. For the importance of giving children skill training, *see* Dobson, *Hide or Seek,* Chapter 4, "Strategy for Esteem," pp. 47–138, especially pp. 69–74.

Chapter 16   **Creativity and Language**

48. For extra "sound fun" ideas, *see* Lillian A. Buckly and Albert Cullum, *Picnic of Sounds: A Playful Approach to Reading* (New York: Citation Press, 1975).
49. For basic background and specific activities, *see* Dr. Harry W. Forgan, *You Can Help Your Child Learn to Read: New Ways to Make Learning Fun* (Toronto: Pagurian Press, 1975).

Chapter 17   **Kids and Good Books**

50. James C. Hefley, "The Charles Paul Conn Story," *Bookstore Journal,* February, 1977.
51. "True" does not mean *nonfiction.* I am not suggesting that you read only nonfiction with your children. A good fairy tale is true in that it

brings into the child's experience some true illumination of human fear or human courage or some trait characteristic of people. When we are looking at fiction work, we must judge truth as to *how true it is to the human condition, how accurately it represents a relevant reality.*

Chapter 18 Creative Thinking

52. My headings follow the sequential development of thought patterns in young children as I have observed them. The headings are based on Benjamin S. Bloom, *Taxonomy of Educational Objectives* (New York: David McKay Co., Inc., 1956).
53. Piaget's interest in the process by which children build up the basic framework of thought has resulted in new understandings in the way in which children's thought patterns develop from infancy. Interested parents can read further: Mary A. Pulaski, *Understanding Piaget: An Introduction to Children's Cognitive Development* (New York: Harper & Row, 1971).
54. *Webster's New Collegiate Dictionary*, definition #1.

Chapter 19 Getting It Together

55. Horatius Bonar, *God's Way of Holiness* (Chicago: Moody Press, n. d.), p. 110.
56. Sy Miller and Jill Jackson, "Let There Be Peace on Earth," Jan-Lee Music.
57. Quoted in Elizabeth O'Connor's book *Eighth Day of Creation* (Waco: Word Books, 1971), p. 101.
58. *Compare* Jesus' parable of the wise and foolish builders in Matthew 7:24–27.

Recommended Reading for Chapter 15 **Creativity and Crafts**

(There are scores of crafts books on the market. Here are some we found to be particularly helpful.)

Lewis, Felicity, *How to Make Presents From Odds and Ends.* New York: Crescent Books, 1972. A little book with a British touch. Fun.
Make and Do. Volume 9 of *Childcraft: The How and Why Library.* Chicago: Field Enterprises Educational Corporation. The basic "textbook" for our children's creative activities; a wide range of suggestions, well organized and illustrated—a book preschoolers can use with very little help.

May, Marian, ed. *Sunset Crafts for Children.* Menlo Park: Lane Books,
1968. A late arrival in our home—but a good resource book for simple
crafts for older preschoolers.

Wiseman, Ann. *Making Things.* Boston: Little, Brown and Company,
1973. Beautiful in design, this hand-lettered book with accompanying
sketches has an abundance of ideas. As a "handbook of creative discovery," it helps parent and child go beyond one craft to another
related one. Most of the projects require help if undertaken by preschoolers.

Withers, Andrew. *How to Make Cards for All Occasions.* New York:
Crescent Books. Another small "how to" book full of nifty ideas on
ways to design, fold, and letter cards.

Index

248

3235

Hancock, Maxine

People in process.

DATE DUE

JUL 1 8 '79			
NOV 2 5 '79			
JUN 1 5 '80			
30 508 JOSTEN'S			